D1096095

Designer Needle Felting

Designer Needle Felting

CONTEMPORARY STYLES, EASY TECHNIQUES

TERRY TAYLOR AND CANDIE COOPER

LARK BOOKS
A Division of Sterling Publishing Co., Inc.
New York / London

Art Director
STACEY BUDGE

Cover Designer
CINDY LABREACHT

Assistant Editors
MARK BLOOM
JULIE HALE

Associate Art Director
LANCE WILLE

Art Production Assistant
JEFF HAMILTON

Illustrator
ORRIN LUNDGREN

Photographer
STEWART O'SHIELDS

Library of Congress Cataloging-in-Publication Data

Taylor, Terry, 1952-
Designer needle felting : contemporary styles, easy techniques / Terry Taylor and Candie Cooper. — 1st ed.
p. cm.
Includes index.
ISBN-13: 978-1-57990-999-4 (hc-plc with jacket : alk. paper)
ISBN-10: 1-57990-999-X (hc-plc with jacket : alk. paper)
1. Felt work. 2. Felting. I. Cooper, Candie, 1979- II. Title.
TT849.5.T39 2007
746'.0463—dc22
2007007840

10 9 8 7 6 5 4 3 2 1

First Edition

Published by Lark Books, A Division of
Sterling Publishing Co., Inc.
387 Park Avenue South, New York, N.Y. 10016

Distributed in Canada by Sterling Publishing,
c/o Canadian Manda Group, 165 Dufferin Street
Toronto, Ontario, Canada M6K 3H6

Distributed in the United Kingdom by GMC Distribution Services,
Castle Place, 166 High Street, Lewes, East Sussex, England BN7 1XU

Distributed in Australia by Capricorn Link (Australia) Pty Ltd.,
P.O. Box 704, Windsor, NSW 2756 Australia

If you have questions or comments about this book, please contact:
Lark Books
67 Broadway
Asheville, NC 28801
(828) 253-0467

Manufactured in China

ISBN 13: 978-1-57990-999-4
ISBN 10: 1-57990-999-X

For information about custom editions, special sales, premium and corporate purchases, please contact Sterling Special Sales Department at 800-805-5489 or specialsales@sterlingpub.com.

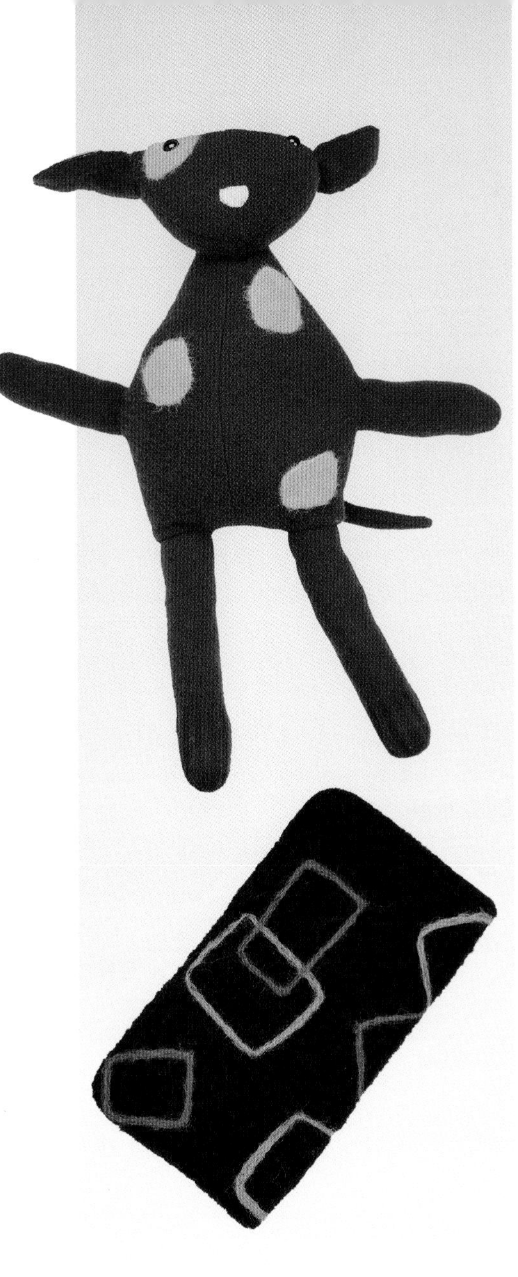

Contents

Introduction

IF YOUR IDEA OF FELT is limited to brightly colored sheets on craft store shelves or perhaps a laundry disaster involving your favorite pair of hand-knit wool socks, let us broaden your horizons. Take a look at the imaginative creations featured in this book, and you'll soon discover the beauty, versatility, and artistic appeal of needle felting.

People have been making felt for centuries. Typically, the process involves two elements—moisture and agitation. (Remember the mishap in the washing machine?) In more modern times, a process called needle felting—also known as dry felting—was developed commercially for making felt yardage. (That's where those brightly colored sheets begin.) This process uses barbed needles instead of water and agitation to entangle wool fibers.

Over the years, fiber artists and crafters have experimented with the needle-felting process to produce a wide range of modern, innovative items. To show you just how fun and sophisticated needle felting can be, we've assembled 25 projects from a team of talented designers. You'll find creative ideas for every skill level, from

beginning to advanced, as well as projects that combine both wet and dry felting techniques.

Browse these pages, and you'll see a range of projects, from stylish clothing and accessories to cool jewelry and household items to whimsical pieces you can make just for the fun of it. One-of-a-kind, wearable creations like the Elegance Personified Evening Sweater and the Tutti Frutti Baubles feature seed beads and colorful fibers, in addition to ingenious designs. Practical yet stylish accessories like the Graphic Eyeglass Cases and the Lollipops Bag highlight the durability of needle felting. There are projects that encourage you to recycle old sweaters, practice your embroidery or knitting stitches, and embellish to your heart's content with sequins, ribbons, beads, and—most of all—wool. Throughout, you can fall in love with needle felting by experimenting with color and form.

If you've never felted with a needle before, then this is the book for you. The basics section covers everything you need to know to get started. It contains information on materials and tools, as well as a rundown of the basic felting techniques you should be familiar with to create these fabulous projects. The basics section will also get you acquainted with varieties of wool and how it becomes felt. Making a sheet of felt is easy, and once you get the hang of it, you'll be ready to tackle all of the fun ideas included here.

Whether you're an experienced felter looking for fresh ideas or someone who's just getting started with the craft, you've come to the right place. So pick out a project, gather your tools and materials, and get ready to felt with a needle!

Needle Felting Basics

Unprocessed fleece and wool locks

MATERIALS

Wool—which comes from sheep—is essential to making felt. Different breeds of sheep produce different types of fiber. Some kinds are extremely coarse, while others are extremely fine. It takes many steps to get wool from a sheep into the consumer's hands. Shorn wool, called fleece, must be picked through to remove bits of dirt and straw. Once this process is complete, the fleece is washed in hot water to rid it of dirt and oil. The fleece is then laid out to dry. At this point, the wool is pretty much the same as it was when still on the sheep, except that now it's clean. The curly or straight pieces of wool are called locks.

After it dries, the wool is put through a carding machine. The carding machine—also known as a carder—combs out the fibers. It transforms the curly locks of wool into either a sheet called a batt or a long, continuous strand called roving. You can make felt from either form of carded wool.

As you begin working with felt, you'll discover that certain fibers work better with wet felting, while others are better suited to needle or dry felting. The felting process hinges on the wool's fiber properties. Each fiber has little microscopic scales that open and close. In traditional wet felting, soap and hot water prompt the opening of the scales: with agitation, pressure, and dish soap (for lubrication and pH factors), the wool's fibers get tangled around each other to create felt.

During the dry-felting process, special felting needles penetrate the wool repeatedly. During this penetration, the barbs on the felting needles latch onto the fibers in the wool, tangling and drawing them together to make felt.

You don't have to choose one form of felting over the other—you can combine wet-felting and dry-felting (also called needle felting) techniques in different and innovative ways to create a variety of fabulous projects.

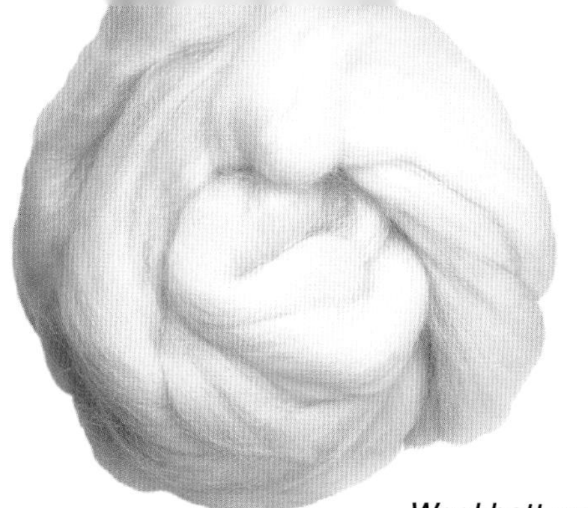

Wool batt and roving

WOOLS FOR FELTING

Try experimenting with different types of wool, so that you can familiarize yourself with all of the unique qualities the material can have. Through fiber stores and websites, you can purchase wools of all kinds and colors, from natural shades to bright hues, from super-soft to coarse.

You can also dye wool yourself to produce unique colors. Interesting novelty fibers like metallic strands or recycled denim scraps can also be blended into your wools. Ultimately, the type of wool you use will depend on the project you're making. One type of wool may be better suited for one project than another. Before purchasing a large quantity of wool, consult with the owner of your local fiber shop or with a fellow felter for a second opinion about your project. Below are some general suggestions about the kinds of wools that work best with needle and wet felting.

Needle Felting Wool

In general, medium to coarse wools work best for needle felting, but all wool can be felted with a needle. Check out the list on this page for information regarding different sheep breeds and uses for their wool. You'll also find specific wools included in the materials lists of the projects in this book.

Wet Felting Wool

Finer wools such as Merino work well for wet felting. Merino creates a soft, smooth felt that can also be great for needle felting. Gotland wool is also conducive to wet felting and makes a very soft felt. For a truly unique surface, try felting mohair locks together—this will produce a soft yet curly, shiny surface. You can experiment with other kinds of wool by wet felting a small test sheet to see whether you like the finished appearance.

HAVE WOOL, WILL FELT

Hampshire *and* **Dorset** *sheep are raised mainly for meat, and as a result, their wool is not readily available. But the coarseness of this type of wool makes it perfect for needle felting, particularly core shapes. Be on the lookout for sheep farmers in your area—ask if you can buy the raw wool, then send it to a processor or prepare it yourself.*

Merino *is a very popular soft wool perfect for needle or wet felting. If Merino wool is needle felted, holes will show on the surface, but those can easily be whisked away with a bit of careful wet felting.*

Romney *and* **Corriedale** *wools are wonderful for needle felting. When felted, these wools tend to look very hairy compared to a smoother wool like Merino.*

Angora goats are covered in curly **mohair** *locks. The locks are very silky and can be wet felted or needle felted. You can purchase them in natural or dyed colors.*

Alpaca *and* **llama** *wools will felt as well. Some folks even use the fur of their pet dogs for felting! You can use these unique fibers as they are, or blend them with other wools to create soft, unique textures.*

BASES FOR NEEDLE FELTING

Polystyrene Foam

A polystyrene foam shape can provide a sturdy core for needle felting wool. The projects on pages 92 and 120 use foam shapes as bases. (That's right—beneath the beautiful layers of wool and embellishments is a polystyrene foam egg!) Use the white porous foam and pre-made foam shapes from the floral section of your local craft store. You can also buy blocks of foam and cut out your own shapes with a serrated knife. Stay away from green florist's foam, because it's too soft and creates a fine dust that will contaminate your wool. If you cut your own shapes, be sure to remove all the bits of foam before felting. Use a hair dryer to blow off the dust and excess pieces.

Fabrics

Wool yardage in tweed, cashmere, houndstooth, and jersey knit can be purchased from your fabric store and used for needle felting. Some fabrics can be felted as they are on the bolt, while others may need to be fulled in the washing machine first. If you aren't sure you like a certain fabric, test a small piece of the material to see whether the finished look appeals to you. If not, remedies such as a different felting needle, a different type of wool, wet felting, or ironing may do the trick.

A few of the projects in this book involve needle felting into a fulled piece of wool or a section of a sweater, as seen on pages 42 and 48. This fulling process is commonly referred to as "felting a sweater." You can find 100 percent wool sweaters or suits at secondhand stores—just check the labels on the garments to make certain they're pure wool before you purchase them. Look for sweaters with ribbed or raised patterns that can result in interesting textures after the material is fulled.

Wool isn't the only base fabric you can use for needle felting. Cottons, denim, and acrylic craft felt work well in needle-felting projects because of their tight weave. It never hurts to experiment with a swatch of fabric. Check the clearance racks at the fabric store for unusual fabrics, such as knit yardage or printed corduroy to embellish with your felting needle and wool.

Purchased Felt Shapes

If you're familiar with felting, you probably already know that you can create your own felt balls using wool, a little soap, and water. But you can also find felt balls in fiber and craft stores or online. The balls come in a variety of colors, and you can decorate them with needle-felted designs or stitching. Felt bracelets, flowers, hearts, and loops are also available and can be used as fun additions to your designs.

EMBELLISHING MATERIALS

Surfaces can be embellished as plainly or as intricately as you like. Fiber and craft stores are full of interesting materials that you can add to your felted surfaces. For example, you can embellish a project by needle felting novelty yarns and wool into the piece, or use other techniques such as hand stitching with beads and sequins. The possibilities are infinite, and you can produce some gorgeous textures. My favorite embellishing materials are listed below.

Embroidery threads, including metallic, satin, and cotton, can be used for decorative stitching on felt surfaces. You can also cut the skeins into confetti-like pieces and sprinkle them onto a pile of wool before wet felting.

Wool and novelty yarns can transform the look of a project. Try needle felting eyelash yarn into felt sheets, balls, or foam forms for a distinctive surface.

Metallic or iridescent fiber strands blended with wool roving or batt will add sparkle to your creations.

Recycled silk yarn (from Nepal) can be shredded and wet felted into place or needle felted for an alternate texture.

Raw fibers such as wool, angora, cotton, and locks can be blended into wool by wet felting or needle felting.

Fabrics or acrylic craft felt cut into small pieces can be appliquéd onto felt surfaces or needle felted.

Silk hankies—try pulling one apart, cobweb-fashion, and laying it over a pile of wool that's ready to be wet or needle felted.

Seed beads and sequins will add a bit of sparkle and pizzazz to any felted surface. These materials come in a range of colors, shapes, and sizes, and can be used one at a time, in multiples, or stacked on top of each other. Seed beads are generally classified by numbers ranging from 15/0 to 1/0—the larger the number, the smaller the bead size.

NEEDLE FELTING TOOLS

FELTING NEEDLES

Warning: *These needles are extremely sharp. Use caution when needle felting, and keep the needles away from children at all times.*

Just as painters use several different types of brushes as they work, needle felters use a variety of needles. The basic felting needle is a 3½- to 4-inch-long (9 to 10 cm) piece of steel wire with a triangular or star-shaped shaft. The shaft has a sharp point and hard-to-see barbs along all the sides. Felting needle sizes are indicated numerically. Different shapes and sizes allow for versatility—some needles are better for certain jobs than others. With practice and experimentation, you'll easily be able to figure out which size works best for a specific task, and which wool types the needles should be paired with. Here's a list of felting needles and their suggested uses:

Single Needles

A 36-gauge triangular felting needle is good for beginning work such as needle felting wool to a precut shape, working with coarse wool, and general sculpting.

A 38-gauge triangular felting needle is a great multitask needle. From the start of a piece to the finishing stages, this is an all-around handy needle.

A 38-gauge star-blade needle is also very versatile in that you can use it to attach yarn or wool to a finished piece or to work the wool in the beginning stages. The difference between this needle and the 38-gauge triangular felting needle is that there are four barbed sides instead of three, which allows you to needle felt the fibers a bit faster.

A 40-gauge triangular felting needle is very fine compared to the first three needles. Because of its small size, this needle is perfect for detailing and embellishing work. It can smooth out a surface if there are pockmarks. It's also handy for adding yarns, silks, and other materials.

Other Types of Felting Needles

Felting needles with special rubberized ends for easy and comfortable gripping can be found on the Internet or in fiber supply shops. These needles cost a bit more than regular felting needles, but they're handy—especially if you're needle felting for long periods—because they provide a better grip.

Multi-needle holders that can accommodate three or more needles at a time are also available. Because they let you cover a lot of space in a short time, multi-needle tools are wonderful for working on pieces with large surface areas, such as a two-dimensional wall piece or a hat. These holders can accommodate needles of all gauges. You can easily change needles, as well.

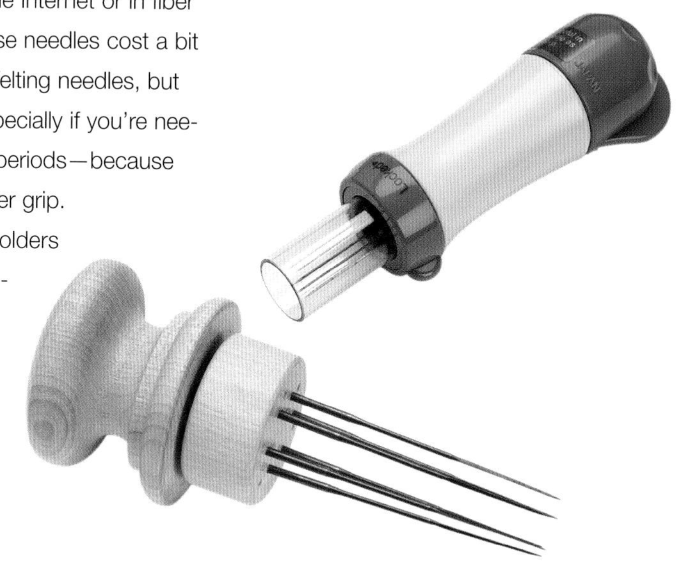

NEEDLE TIPS

Store your needles in a candy or mint container to keep them from getting broken.

Needles are brittle, so keep a couple of spare sets on hand in case you break a set while needle felting.

Store your needles in a dry area—they can easily rust.

To prevent painful accidents, dispose of broken needles appropriately.

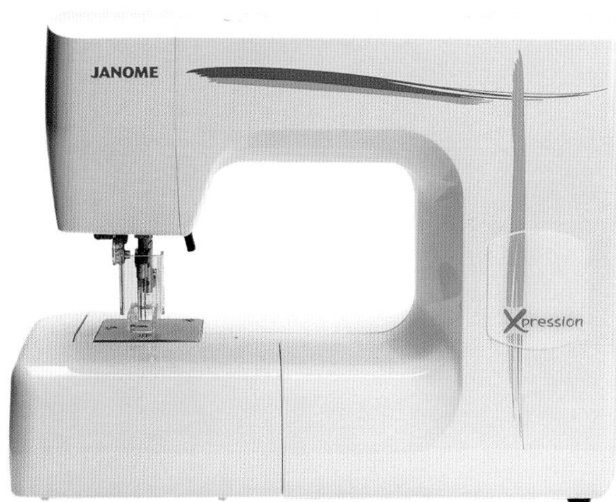

Needle-felting machine

NEEDLE-FELTING MACHINES

A needle-felting machine works in much the same way as a multi-needle holder, except that the machine does all the work. The machine contains several felting needles. The needles push the fibers into the base fabric, and you control the fabric feed. You can needle felt much more quickly with a machine. It's a wonderful tool for embellishing pre-made garments and household items with novelty yarns, wool scraps, threads, roving, or fabrics.

WORK SURFACES FOR NEEDLE FELTING

Before you get started on a project, set up your workspace. A table covered with one of the following materials is ideal for needle felting.

Upholstery Foam

High-density foam about 2 inches (5.1 cm) thick makes a great surface for needle felting. The foam will support the piece you're working on and keep the needles from breaking. Inexpensive upholstery foam scraps or chair pads are available at fabric supply stores. Foam forms made especially for needle felting hats and purses are also available, although you can easily saw or carve the foam into a special shape with a serrated knife to suit specific project needs. Keep in mind that the foam will get brittle with use and need to be replaced. To remove stray fibers from the foam, use a sticky lint brush.

You may decide to needle felt purposefully into a piece of upholstery foam or polystyrene foam. Instead of pulling your wool away from the foam, you'll be pushing it down into the pores of the foam with the felting needle. The foam thus becomes a permanent work surface that will end up as a decoration.

Brush Block

The brush block is a new type of needle-felting work surface. A brush block looks a lot like a large scrub brush. It has a base that sits on the work surface and stiff bristles that point upward. The bristles are dense enough to provide adequate support for your wool and tall enough to keep needles from making contact with the base and breaking. You can remove loose fibers from the bristles with a comb.

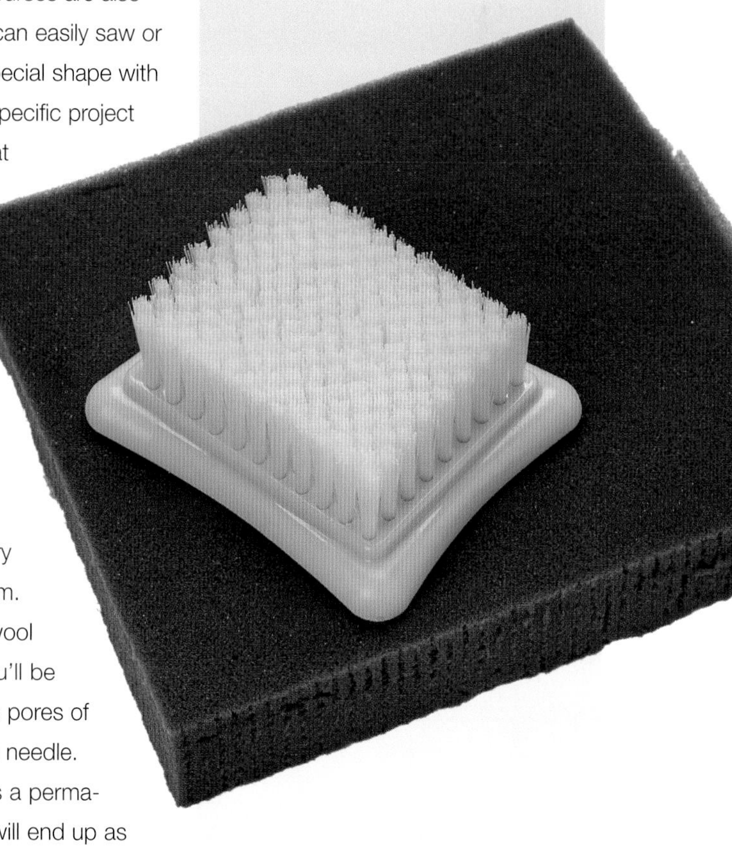

OTHER TOOLS

Scissors

Fabric scissors are useful for cutting out felt pieces and wool fabric. Small, sharp scissors come in handy for snipping threads.

Needles

When working with fibers, it's good to have a variety of needles on hand. A straight upholstery or tapestry needle is key when stringing felted pieces, because the eye of the needle is big enough to accommodate the wire. A basic sewing needle for embellishing wool surfaces with embroidery or seed beads is also useful.

FELTING TECHNIQUES

Although this book focuses on the magic of needle felting, we've also included some basic information on wet felting so that you'll have another creative option when working with wool. The technique you choose will depend on the look you want for the finished piece. Needle felting and wet felting are related, but they're very different. To get a feel for each technique, try experimenting with small pieces of fabric. The most important thing to remember is that there are no strict rules here. Have fun and let your imagination take over!

PREPARING WOOL FOR FELTING

Splitting Wool Roving

Roving is wool that's been washed and then carded (meaning that the fibers have been cleaned, separated, and straightened) into long, rope-like lengths or rolls. To pull off a length of wool and split it, you must first divide the roving up widthwise. Place your hand 8 or more inches (20 cm) from the end of the roving, and pull a length of wool from the roll with your other hand. Then split that piece lengthwise into smaller, thinner segments. These small pieces are called slivers.

Blending Different Colors of Wool Together

Small amounts of two different colors of wool can easily be blended by hand. When felted, the swirling colors of fiber create a beautiful effect, as seen in the Autumn Leaves Runner to the left.

To blend two different colors of wool, start by tearing off two 6-inch (15.2 cm) lengths of wool of each color, and then lay one piece on top of the other. Grab the pieces by each end and pull them apart. Next, lay these two pieces on top of each other and repeat the process until you're happy with the overall blend.

NEEDLE FELTING

One of the great benefits of needle felting is that you have more control over the fiber than you do when wet felting (see page 19 for information on wet felting). If you make a mistake while needle felting, you can simply erase it by pulling the piece of wool off and starting again.

When punching into wool with a felting needle, the bottom ¾-inch (1.9 cm) barbed section of the needle does the work. As you punch in and out of the wool, the barbs latch onto the fibers, repeatedly picking them up and then dropping them. Sometimes you'll punch deeply into the wool with the needle. Other times, you'll use just the tip of the needle to penetrate the surface. It all depends on the type of project you're making. Felting needles will also change with the type of task you're completing—some needles are good for general sculpting, while others are good for detail work. For more information on felting needles, check out the Tools section on page 12.

As you needle felt, insert the needle into the wool, and then bring the needle back up and out of the same hole it went into initially. Always move the needle in a straight up-and-down motion. The needle in your hand moves just the way it would on a sewing machine—in and out, up and down. As you progress, resist the temptation to use the felting needle to pull the wool over to a certain spot. This can lead to a broken needle.

FELTING TIPS

Pay attention to your project at all times! Try not to felt in front of the TV—you may get distracted and stab yourself.

Take breaks from needle felting to stretch. This will keep you from getting cramps.

Pull your piece from the work surface often to ensure that it doesn't get attached.

Working in Two Dimensions

Needle Felting a Flat Sheet of Wool. To make a flat sheet of felt by needle felting, start by tearing off six to eight small, even-length tufts of wool. Position two pieces of wool side by side on your work surface so that the edges of each piece just barely overlap one another.

Lay two more pieces on top, in the same fashion, but position these pieces so that they're perpendicular to the first layer. The next layer should be laid out perpendicular to the second layer. Take care when laying out the wool that there are no holes or thin spots. Fill in any thin areas with a small, wispy tuft of wool. The number of layers determines the thickness of the finished wool sheet. Start with three or four layers—you can always add more layers later.

Next, poke the layers of wool with your felting needle in a straight up-and-down fashion. A multi-needle felting tool can come in handy here, as it will speed up your felting time considerably. Gently pull the piece off the work surface from time to time to prevent it from getting too deeply enmeshed in the foam or bristles (see Work Surfaces for Needle Felting on page 13). Loose edges of wool can be folded over and felted into the piece. You can needle felt both sides of the sheet as well. If you decide your piece of felt is too thin, simply add a couple of extra layers as you did when you initially laid out your wool and continue needle felting.

Crisscross the layers of roving.

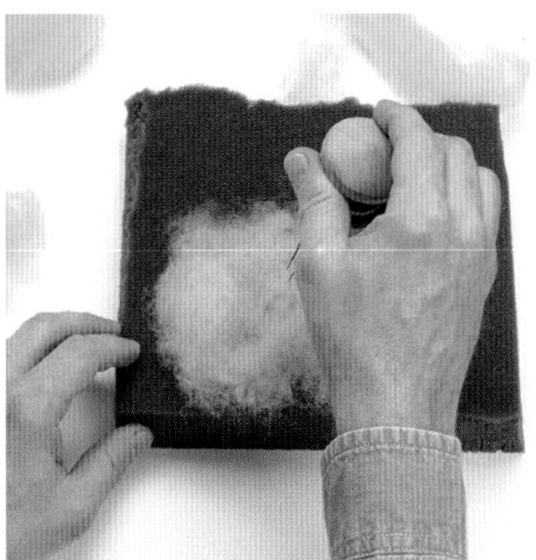

A multi-needle tool speeds the felting process.

Needle Felting into a Base Fabric Shape. Another fun way to needle felt is to cut a shape out of a good base fabric and needle felt wool onto it. The base fabric serves as a template or a guide, making it easy to create a specific shape as you work. Simply place the fabric shape face up on top of your work surface, and lay out tufts of wool that roughly fit into the shape. Then poke the wool into the shape, making sure it's covered evenly. Continue building up a thick layer of wool. You can also add a thin layer on the back side to cover the base fabric. If the sides don't look round enough, tack some wool on the front and bring the opposite end around to the back, and felt it in. You can see a variation of this technique in the Passel of Puppy Pins project on page 86.

Needle-Punch or Felting Machine. If you have used a multi-needle tool to attach layers to a base fabric, then you can pretty much imagine the possibilities of what a needle-punch machine can do. Base fabric and fiber of all sorts along with this machine can create ultra-rich textures for wearables or home decor.

As mentioned in the materials section (see page 10), felt, denim, and cottons work well as base fabrics. Position your fibers, be they roving, yarns, scraps of wool, or anything else, on top of the base fabric. If you choose to pin your fibers in place, take care not to run over the pins with the felting needles. Put your piece into place below the needles and use the pedal to control the needle action and your hands to control the fabric feed.

Working in Three Dimensions

Believe it or not, fluffy wool can actually be sculpted into a solid, three-dimensional object. You can needle felt the wool by itself or felt it into polystyrene or upholstery foam core shapes (see Polystyrene Foam on page 10). Using only wool, your objects can be super-dense or light and airy—it all depends on the amount of poking you do with your needle. Try using less expensive wool for your core shape, then covering it with dyed wool. For example, you could build a doll using neutral-colored wool, and then add clothing by needle felting dyed wool onto the body.

A good way to approach three-dimensional needle felting is to break your design into parts. Let's go back to the doll example. You would have to needle felt each body part—torso, head, legs, and arms—separately. Since these parts can easily be translated into simple forms like tubes, spheres, and ovals, the task isn't as difficult as it might sound. Try to keep your shapes on the fluffy side rather than stiff and dense, which will make it easier to connect the parts. Once the pieces are joined, you can needle felt the assemblage further, as a whole.

Tear off a piece of roving and roll it into the desired shape—a tube, for instance, or an oval. Work on a non-skid surface like upholstery foam, so you can keep the center snug and tight. For sphere shapes, such as a bead or a head, try tying a knot at one end of the roving and then wrapping the wool around the knot. Don't let go of the rolled piece because it can easily unwind. Use a felting needle to tack the piece in place as you roll. If you're happy with the dimensions of the shape and have too much wool, simply pull the excess away with your spare hand while holding on to the core piece. Don't use scissors to remove the extra wool—a bluntly cut edge won't blend into the rest of the piece as nicely as a torn edge will.

Roving rolled into a tubular shape.

Once you've finished rolling, poke the shape with the felting needle in different directions. You'll find that the wool will move in the direction you poke it, so if a piece is too tall or too long, poke it with the felting needle to draw it in. Take care not to poke the felting needle in so deeply that it comes out the other side of the piece. If you feel the piece is too small, don't worry—you can always wrap more wool around it and continue needle felting.

Many needle-felted shapes can be connected to each other with a felting needle. Start with the biggest shape and connect the smaller pieces to it. Position the small piece where you want it, then poke through the two pieces, angling the felting needle in different directions to make a secure connection. If, after needle felting, you don't like the placement, simply pull the two pieces apart, reposition them, and start again. A small tuft of wool can be wrapped around the joint area and felted to conceal the connection. Depending on your design, a wispy area of wool can be intentionally left on the piece. This wispy section can then be spread across an area of the base and needle felted into place. For finer details, such as fingers or cheeks, fold and roll some small tufts of wool, then needle felt them into place.

Covering a Polystyrene Foam Shape

You can needle felt wool into a piece of polystyrene or upholstery foam, as seen in the Easter Eggs project on page 120. Polystyrene foam is sturdy, while upholstery foam is soft. You can create your own foam shapes by blocking out your design on the foam with a permanent marker, then using a serrated knife to carefully carve out the piece.

Wool in roving or batt form can be used to cover the shape. Roving is easiest to use because it can be wound in one continuous piece around the shape. Put a piece of cardboard underneath your foam shape before you begin working, because the needles may leave marks on your tabletop. Find your starting point on the foam, then place the end of your roving there. If you're working with a wool batt, lay it over the area you want to cover. Depending on the size of your piece, you can use a single or a multi-needle tool on the foam. Many pokes with the needle will produce a tight, smooth surface, while fewer pokes will produce a fluffier surface. You can add as many layers of wool as you wish. Novelty yarns and fibers can be needle felted into the core, too. For added sparkle, try stringing beads and sequins onto straight pins and gluing them in place.

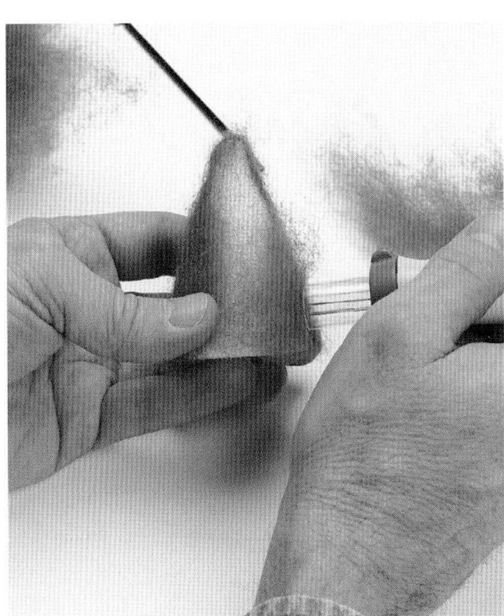

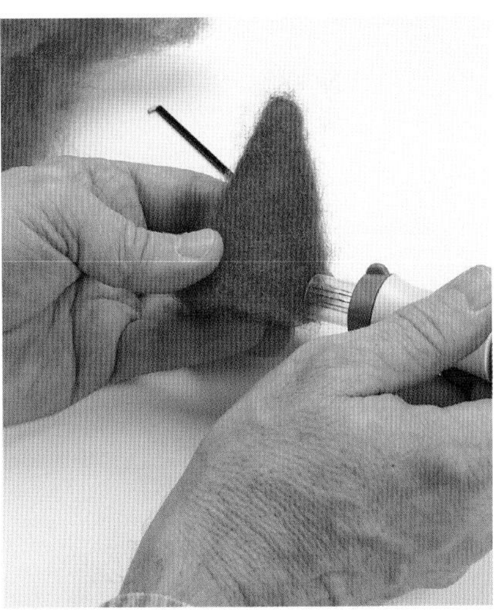

EMBELLISHING

Adding Designs to a Flat Sheet of Felt

You can add imagery very easily to sheets of felt. The designs can be as simple as a coloring book page or as complex as an impressionistic painting. You can needle felt roving and other fibers to a sheet of felt with a single needle or multi-needle tool. This is where different gauges of felting needles come into play, because certain needles will respond better to the task and to the fiber than others will.

You can split or twist the wool roving to create skinny, detailed lines, or use the roving as it is to create thick lines and blocks of color. Fewer pokes with the needle will produce a raised surface. It's worth mentioning that there is no "right" or "wrong" side to a needle-felted sheet. You may like the appearance of one side better than the other.

You can adhere pieces cut from other felt sheets and fabrics to your sheet by placing the piece on top and needle felting it to the base. (Note: Always needle felt on your special work surface, so that the needles have a soft place to land.) Decorated sheets such as these can then be wet felted for a laminated effect (see page 20 for information about wet felting a needle-felted object).

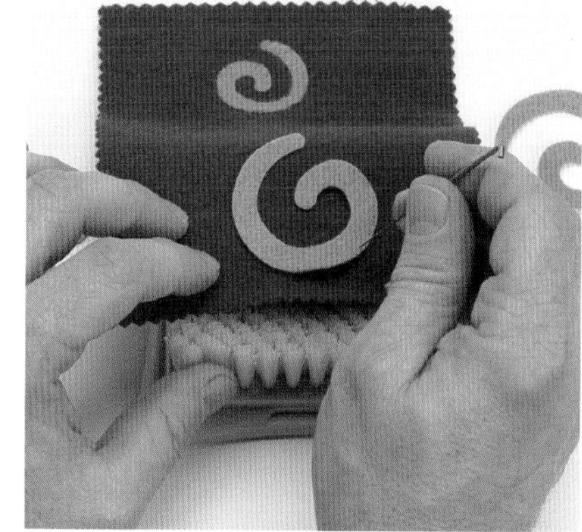

Use a single needle tool to tack a felt shape into place.

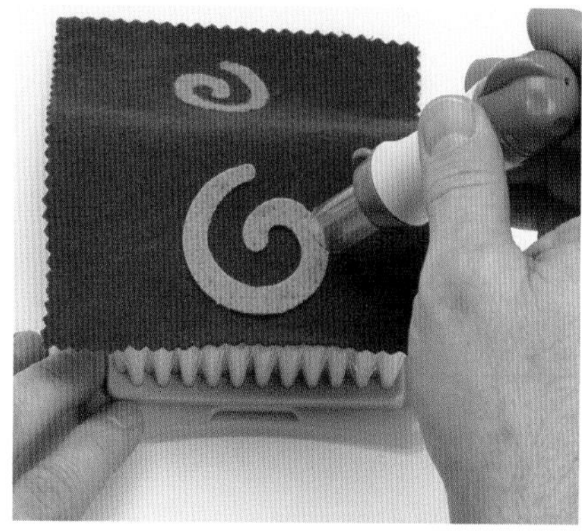

Using a multi-needle will speed up the needle felting process.

Needle Felting into a Base Fabric

Some of the projects in this book—the Cozy Blanket on page 31, for example—embellish pre-made objects with needle felting. Also, you don't have to limit yourself to working on wool or felt; your base fabrics can be cotton and denim. You can embellish these base fabrics easily with wool, novelty fibers, or even cut fabric. No threads or sewing needles are required. Just lay your pieces on top of the base fabric and punch through the two layers with your felting needle. The fibers from the two pieces will become entangled, making a bond. If you experiment, you'll find that some fabrics work better than others with this technique. The use of a needle-felting machine or multi-needle tool can make the process go faster, depending on the complexity of the design (see page 13 for information on using a needle-felting machine).

Pattern and Stencil Options

For a specific shape, try using a cookie cutter as a stencil. You can find cookie cutters of all shapes and sizes in kitchen supply stores or in the polymer clay section of most craft stores.

Simply lay the cookie cutter on

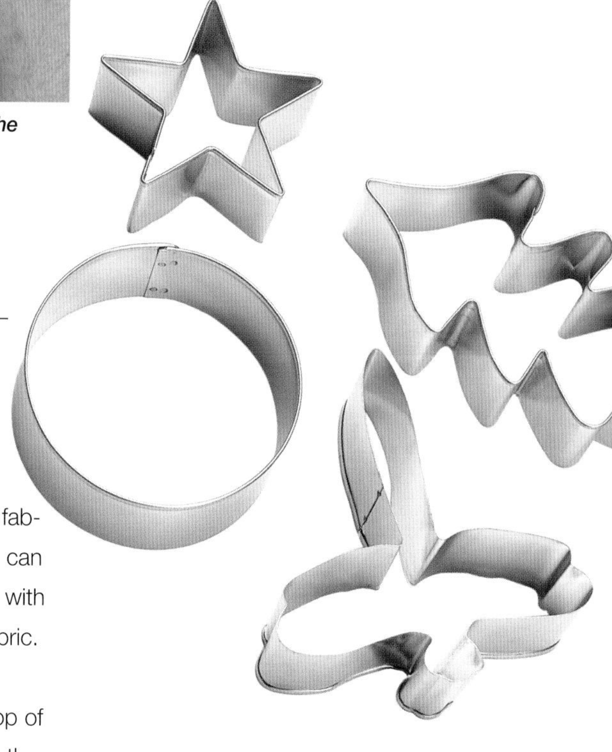

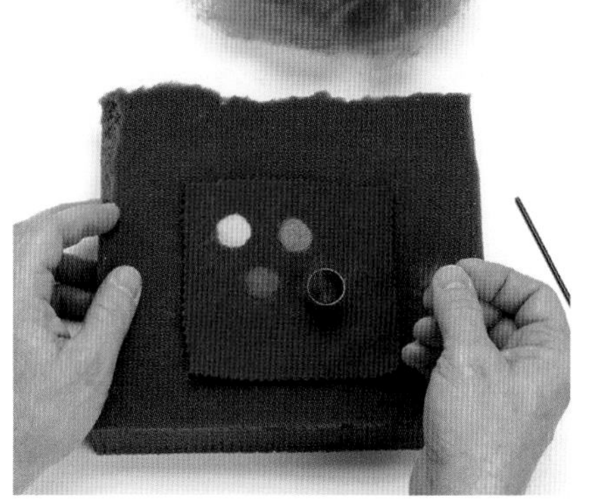

Start with a small amount of wool.

Remove the cutter to neaten the edge of your shape.

your work surface or base fabric. Fill the inside of the cookie cutter with a thin, even layer of wool. Poke your felting needle into the wool next to the wall of the cookie cutter and continue around the perimeter of the shape to secure the outline. Fold any loose edges in toward the center of the shape and needle felt them into place.

Next, work the middle of the design with the felting needle. At this point, you can add more wool and needle felt as you did before, making the design puff up from the surface. You can also try filling the cookie cutter with yarns, silks, or a new color of wool and needle felting the material into the shape.

TROUBLESHOOTING TIPS

When you make a mistake: It's possible to erase mistakes by backtracking—just grab the tail of the wool that's connected to the piece, pull the wool off, and start again. You can also fix problems by adding more wool.

Pockmarks: Those small holes left by the felting needle in the surface of your material are known as pockmarks; 36-gauge needles are notorious for leaving trails of these tiny holes. Sometimes the combination of fiber and needle can lead to problems, so it never hurts to experiment with these elements.

To get rid of pockmarks, try working over the piece with a fine needle, such as a 40-gauge needle. Skimming the surface of the piece with this needle can clear up the holes. Wet felting the piece will also remove pockmarks. See page 20 for information on how to wet felt a needle-felted object.

WET FELTING

A little bit of knowledge about wet felting is very useful so that you can combine the technique with needle felting. Agitation, some soapy water, and wool are all that you need to wet felt. If you've ever accidentally washed a wool sweater, you're probably aware of the shrinkage that can result. When washed in hot water, wool can draw up in size anywhere from 33 to 45 percent, depending on the type of fiber. When laying out your wool, remember that it will be half its original size after it's felted.

Making a Sheet of Felt

Tear a 10-inch (25.4 cm) length of wool roving from the ball and split the length in half. Then tear off small, even-length tufts of wool from the two halves and lay them side by side in the same direction on a rubber mat, making sure that the edges just barely overlap one another.

Lay a second layer of wool on top of the first layer, perpendicular to it. The third layer should then be laid out perpendicular to the second one, and so on. Make sure there are no holes in the piece as you work (if you can still see the rubber mat, do a little more layering). Three or four even layers of wool are usually sufficient to make a standard sheet of felt. As you practice making these sheets, you'll learn what works for you, and how thick you want your felt to be.

Note the size of your wool before you begin wet felting. Later, when you're checking to see whether the

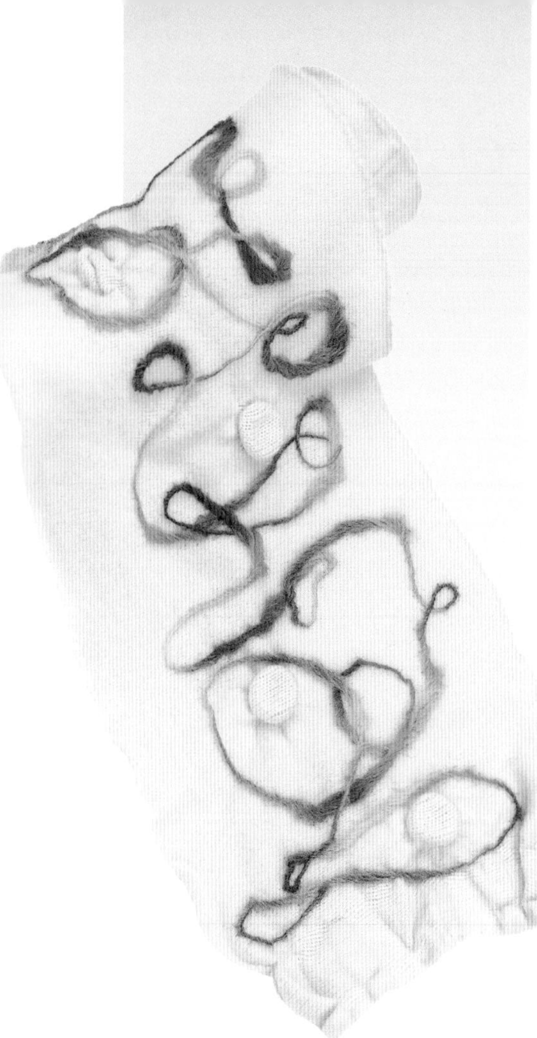

piece is fully felted, the size will serve as an indicator—the piece should be roughly half its original size after felting.

Start the wet-felting process by drizzling some warm soapy water over the layers of wool. Then add a few drops of dish soap. Make sure your hands are wet and soapy as you pat the wool's surface, pushing out bubbles and checking to see that the wool is totally saturated. Soak up any standing water with a sponge. Make small, circular motions with your hands, taking care not to disturb the layers. This step may take several minutes, so be patient. A layer of bubble wrap, bubble side down, is also good to use for rubbing.

Once the fibers feel like they are strong enough to be moved, turn the piece over and rotate it 90°. You can add more pressure as the piece shrinks and strengthens, but make sure the piece remains slippery and wet. Otherwise, the wool may start to pill or make "fuzzies" on its surface. Avoid felting the wool in standing water.

The next step in the process is called fulling. Fulling is intense agitation. To achieve this, roll up your piece like a scroll, then roll it back and forth on the rubber mat. Next, dunk the piece in hot soapy water and lay it out flat on the mat. Then roll up the piece like a scroll in the opposite direction, and roll it back and forth again on the mat. Repeat this process for all four sides.

You'll know when a piece is fully felted by checking the size and checking to see whether there are any loose layers. Do this by trying to pull the sides of the sheet apart—you shouldn't be able to. Continue felting until there are no loose layers, and you have a strong piece of felt. There are no hard and fast rules that say you must wet felt to this point, however. Loosely felted pieces can also be used for needle felting, and you can always wet felt the pieces further, if you like.

Once you've finished wet felting, rinse the piece in cool water and let it dry.

TIP

You should never needle felt into a wet piece of felt. The process simply doesn't work well on wet material.

Wet Felting Needle-Felted Objects

You can easily wet felt a piece that has been needle felted, but keep in mind that doing so will change the surface appearance and size of the piece. Wet felting will also tighten the fibers considerably, causing the piece to shrink. Two-dimensional pieces can be wet felted by simply laying the piece on a rubber mat and saturating it with warm soapy water. You can then use bubble wrap as an agitator.

Fulling Woven or Knit Wool Yardage

A few of the projects in this book involve needle felting into a fulled knit bag, wool suit, or sweater. You can easily turn woven or knit wool fabric into felt—just let your washing machine do the work!

To full the wool yardage, set your washing machine for a small load, on hot. Then add a bit of laundry soap (maybe one-quarter of what you would normally use) and the wool fabric, shut the lid, and let the machine do its thing.

A swatch of knit material from a sweater and a fulled sample.

A portion of a wool skirt and a sample of fulled fabric.

When the washer is finished, you can check to make sure the wool is completely fulled by making a small cut with scissors to see whether the threads unravel. If the threads are still loose, wash the wool again. When the fabric has completely fulled, you can dry it in the dryer on low. And lastly, don't forget to clean the lint trap!

SURFACE EMBELLISHMENTS

There are endless possibilities and combinations for decorating felt surfaces. Fabrics, threads, sequins, novelty fibers, and beads are just the tip of the iceberg when it comes to embellishments. Once you begin felting, you can concoct your own unique ideas. Here are a few to help you get started.

Using Embroidery Stitches

Embroidery stitches can be used to add fantastic details to your felted work. Simple stitches can produce fun surfaces, while more elaborate stitches can be used to create a sophisticated look. Try using different types of threads, such as pearl cotton or metallic threads. Strands of embroidery floss can also be used—try dividing up a strand. Check out embroidery stitch encyclopedias for interesting stitches. Practice the stitch on a scrap of fabric before applying it to the actual piece. You don't want to have to rip out stitches and risk damaging the felt surface.

When embroidering, try not to tug on the needle and thread. Felt pieces sometimes have a porous surface. If you pull too hard on the thread, small stitches can get lost, and long stitches can be reduced to short stitches. You should pull just hard enough on the needle and thread so that the stitches sit on top of the felt. The stitches should be neither too loose nor too tight.

Anchoring the Thread. Before you begin sewing and embellishing on your felt surface, you must first anchor the thread. One way to anchor your thread is by tying a knot at the end of the thread and bringing your needle through to the front so the knot catches on the back of the fabric. Another way is to thread the needle with the desired thread and secure it to the felt surface by making two forward stitches and one backstitch.

If you're embellishing a felt sheet, you can easily anchor your thread to the back side of the fabric. Anchoring thread to a felt ball is a little trickier, but with careful planning, you can find a discreet spot and possibly cover it with a bead or stitch later if it shows.

Here are a few simple stitches to get you started:

Straight Stitches. You can use a straight stitch in multiple ways. To make a straight stitch, tie a knot in the thread and pass it up through the back of the fabric where you want the stitch to begin. Then pass it down through the top of the fabric where you want the stitch to end and then back up where you want the next stitch to begin.

A running stitch is another form of straight stitch, but it produces a dashed line. To make a running stitch, bring the thread over and then under, then back over, and so forth. You can also make asterisks and Xs with a straight stitch.

Chain Stitch. To make a basic chain stitch, tie a knot and pass the thread up through the back of the fabric. Make a loose stitch in the fabric, beginning and ending close to the same point. Leave the thread loose on the top so that it makes a loop. Make the loop as long as you want your chain. Holding the loop with your finger, pass the thread back up through the fabric at point A (see diagram A) and pull the thread until the loop tightens, but not so tight that it pulls the fabric. Repeat the stitch for each link in the chain, keeping each link the same length. At the end of the chain, take a small stitch to hold the last loop in place (see diagram B).

Lazy Daisy Stitch. The lazy daisy stitch is similar to the basic chain except the stitch remains separate instead of being connected to the other stitches. This stitch is often used for making patterns that look like flower petals (see diagram C).

To make a lazy daisy stitch, repeat the steps for making a chain stitch, but do not make the second loop. Instead, make one straight stitch over what would be the wide end of the petal. Then poke the needle through to the place where you want the next petal to start (see diagram D).

Diagram A

Diagram B

Diagram C

Diagram D

French Knot. A French knot is a small, knotted stitch that resembles a seed bead. French knots can add a great deal of texture to a felt surface depending on how closely they're spaced.

To make a French knot, anchor the thread on the surface. Holding the needle in one hand, use your other hand to wrap the thread around the needle two or three times. Then position the tip of the needle next to the place where the thread came up and pull the wrapped thread to remove all the gaps. Poke the needle down through the fabric and don't let go of the wrapped thread end until you've pulled the needle through and removed all of the slack, creating a secure stitch. See diagrams E and F.

Whipstitch. A whipstitch can be used to stitch a small felt piece to a larger felt piece. It can also serve as a decorative edge on a piece of fabric (see diagram G).

To make a whipstitch, anchor the thread on the back of the small felt piece and bring the needle up through the front of the piece. Then poke the needle back down through the middle of the large felt piece and up through the small piece, just down from where the last stitch started. This creates a little gap between the stitches. Repeat this stitch around the border of the small piece, and then anchor the thread on the back again.

Try variations of these stitches. Experiment by zigzagging a stitch or mixing two or three different kinds of stitches. How about adding some beads within the stitches?

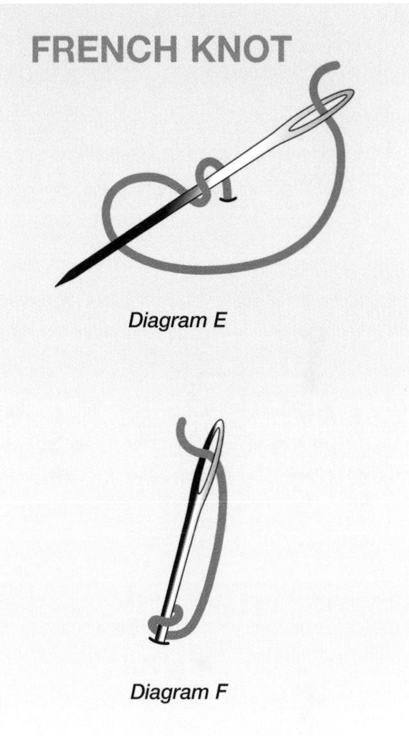

Diagram E

Diagram F

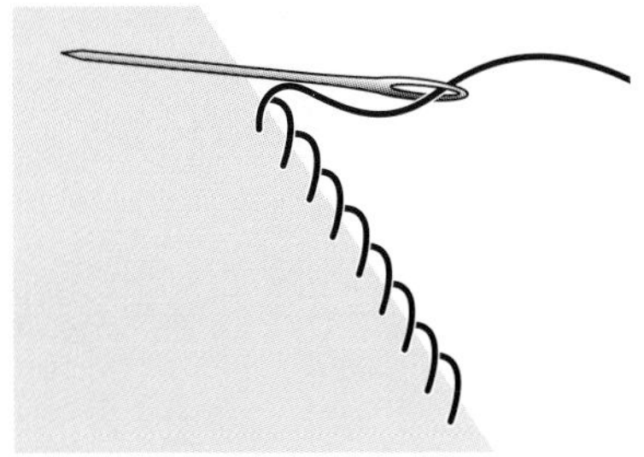

Diagram G

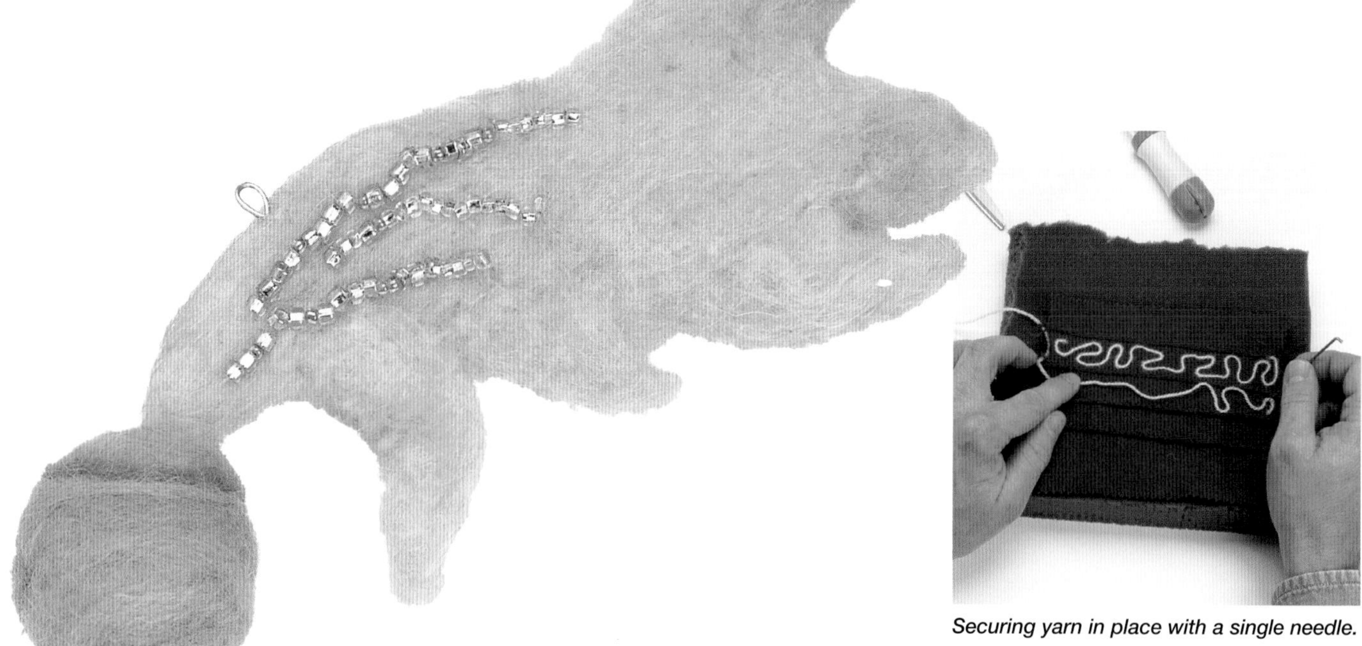

Securing yarn in place with a single needle.

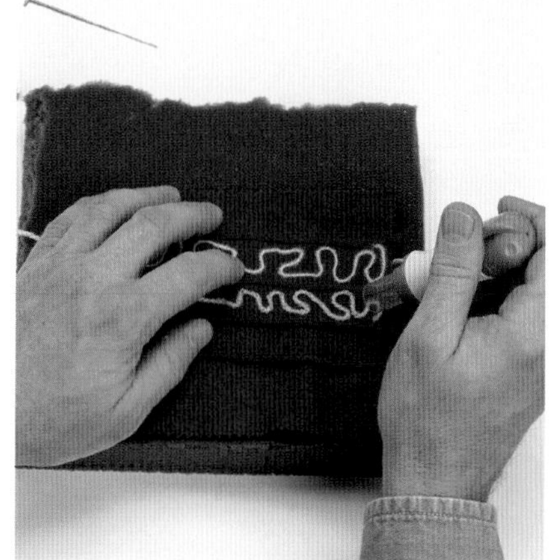

Securing yarn in place with a multi-needle tool.

Seed Beads and Sequins

Before you begin working with beads and sequins, make sure the needle you plan to use fits through the holes in these materials. Thread one bead over the needle and onto the thread, and then insert the needle close to the place where you started. Angle the needle so that it comes up close to where you want to place your next bead. String one sequin followed by a seed bead, and then thread the needle back through the hole in the sequin so that the seed bead holds the sequin in place. Anchor the thread as you did when you started, and trim the end.

Appliqué

You can stitch other fabric pieces onto felt surfaces using a straight stitch. Stitch on small circles of wool or cotton print with an outline or by making small, hidden stitches and turning the edges of the fabric under.

Yarns

All kinds of yarn can be needle felted into wool pieces for added embellishment. Novelty yarns make for some very interesting textures.

Simply place the end of the yarn in the spot where your design starts and begin needle felting. A finer needle—a 38- or 40-gauge—is useful for securing the yarns in place. If you want to speed up the process after you've secured the yarns in place, use a multi-needle tool. Some yarns look very different once they've been needle felted into place, so experiment on a scrap piece of felt before committing to your real project. You will also find that some materials take a little more effort to work in than others.

Locks

Add a whimsical touch by needle felting locks into your projects. You can work in the end of a lock or add the entire thing depending on the type of texture you want. Again, a 38- or 40-gauge needle will do the trick for needle felting locks in place.

Locks around the Celestial Sun.

SPECIAL NOTE FOR EMBELLISHING FELT BALLS

Felt balls require a little care when needle felting into them. It's ideal if the ball is a little soft and squishy to ease the needle-felting process and to avoid a lot of broken needles. Felting needles are very brittle and can snap easily, especially when felting a design into a hard felt ball.

Most of the commercial felt balls fit the "squishy" bill. However, if you roll your own, wet felt the ball three-quarters of the way, stop, and let it dry. Once the design is in place, you can finish it by wet felting or needle felting.

Wet felting can alter the appearance of the needle-felted design, so if you want it to stay exactly the same, then you must wet felt the piece to the desired density and then needle felt. To avoid a pile of broken needles, try to insert the needle into a place and bring it back out as straight as it went in.

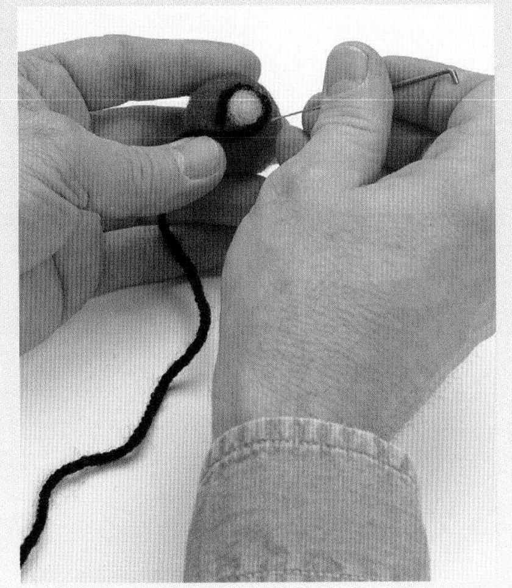

Embellish a felt ball with yarn or roving. Tack the design in place with a single needle tool.

Hearth and Home Projects

Needle felting often begins as a home project, so why shouldn't your creations end up in your home as well? In the following pages, you'll learn how to craft colorful accents to warm almost any room. Turn a plain old blanket into a playful excuse to snuggle up with a loved one. Add some bubble pillows, and you may never want to leave the sofa.

LINDSAY OBERMEYER
designer

Bubble Pillows

SKILL LEVEL
Beginner

FELTING METHOD USED
Dry Felting

FINISHED MEASUREMENTS
15 x 15 inches
(38.1 x 38.1 cm)

WHAT YOU NEED

Marking chalk or pen

Ruler or yardstick

100% wool handmade felt in black, 16 x 24 inches (40.6 x 61 cm)

100% wool Spanish felt in black, 18 x 18 inches (45.7 x 45.7 cm)

Scissors

Wool roving in natural, 48 inches (121.9 cm)

Upholstery foam, 16 x 16 x 3 inches (or larger) (40.6 x 40.6 x 7.6 cm)

40-gauge felting needle

38-gauge star felting needle

Pins

1 skein of 100% wool yarn in cream or natural

Sewing machine

Polyester pillow batting

Black thread (cotton-wrapped polyester)

If you're looking for a quick way to update your living room, these cushions are a cool solution. Make them in black and white, or use colorful fibers that coordinate with your home furnishings.

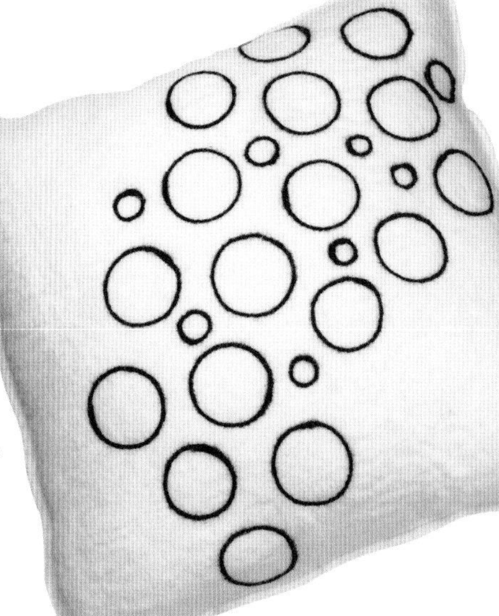

WHAT YOU DO

1 Using the marking chalk and ruler to guide you, measure a 15½-inch (39.4 cm) square from the handmade felt and a 15-inch (38.1 cm) square from the Spanish felt.

2 Cut a 5-inch (12.7 cm) piece of the roving, and then split it in half. Roll one half into a loose ball and lay the second half over the ball.

3 Lay the handmade felt on the upholstery foam and position the mass of roving approximately 2½ to 3 inches (6.4 to 7.6 cm) from the upper left corner of the handmade felt.

4 Begin needle felting with the 40-gauge needle. Work along the edge of the mass, tucking in edges as you go. Remember to occasionally rotate the black felt square to prevent it from sticking to the foam.

5 Once you've firmly tacked down the edges, continue with the center. When it's fairly matted, switch to the 38-gauge star needle. Continue until the circle is dense and firmly attached. If there is a spot with black peeking through, add more roving to the surface and needle felt it into place.

6 Repeat steps 2 through 5 to create a second circle in the upper right corner and a third circle in the lower middle portion of the square. The three dots form a triangle.

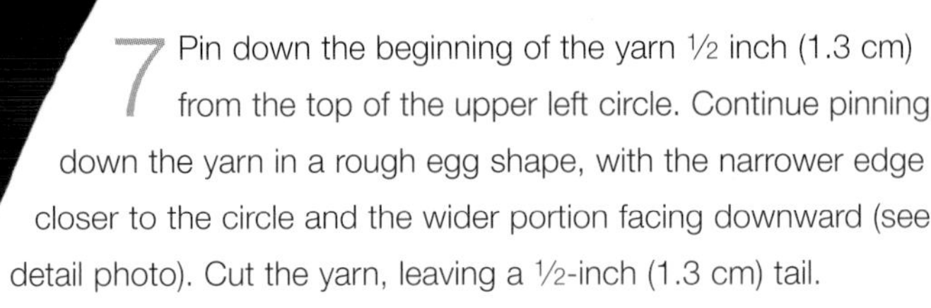

7 Pin down the beginning of the yarn ½ inch (1.3 cm) from the top of the upper left circle. Continue pinning down the yarn in a rough egg shape, with the narrower edge closer to the circle and the wider portion facing downward (see detail photo). Cut the yarn, leaving a ½-inch (1.3 cm) tail.

8 Using the 40-gauge needle, begin loosely needle felting the yarn around the entire circumference. If the shape looks smooth and curvilinear, continue to felt until the yarn is firmly attached.

9 Switch to the 38-gauge star needle and continue felting. Felt down the tail of the yarn, overlapping the beginning. Remove the pins.

10 Repeat steps 7 through 9 for the upper right circle and the lower circle. For the lower circle, pin down the wider portion of the egg shape on an angle to the right instead of facing downward.

11 Repeat steps 7 through 9 to make five 1-inch-diameter (2.5 cm) circles sprinkled across the pillow's surface.

12 Place the handmade felt right side down, and then center the Spanish felt square, right side up, on top of it. Pin the two surfaces together with the black thread, leaving a 3-inch (7.6 cm) gap for the stuffing. Machine- or hand-sew together the two pieces, leaving the gap. Remove the pins.

13 Stuff the pillow with the batting, being certain to push it into the corners. Pin the gap and sew it closed. Then carefully trim the handmade felt to the edge of the Spanish felt.

This project was completed with:

A Child's Dream Come True 100% wool handmade felt in black

A Child's Dream Come True 100% wool Spanish felt in black

Wistyria 100% wool roving in Natural (#100)

Cascade 220 100% highland wool yarn in Cream/Natural (#8010)

Cozy Blanket

designer
LISA CRUSE

What could be cozier than a soft throw embellished with this fabulous border? Use this easy scroll design to enhance your favorite blanket.

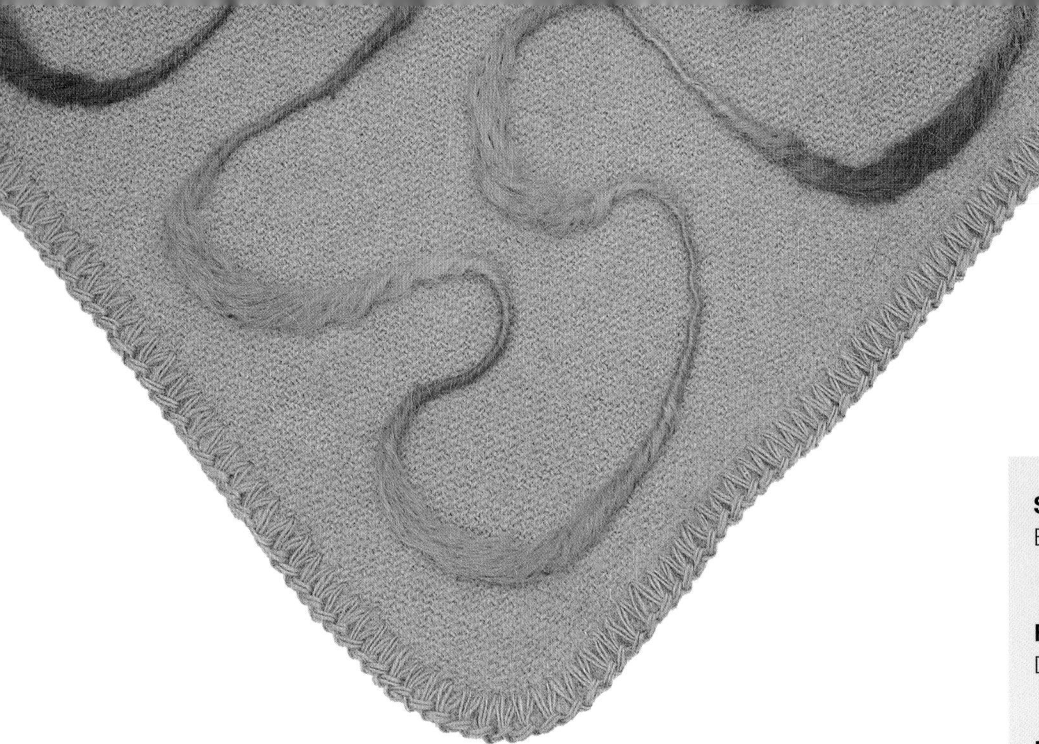

SKILL LEVEL
Beginner

FELTING METHOD USED
Dry Felting

FINISHED MEASUREMENTS
90 x 90 inches (228.6 x 228.6 cm)

WHAT YOU NEED

- Wool throw, any size (the sample used here is 90 inches [228.6 cm] square), preferably a solid color
- Tape measure or ruler
- Dressmaker's pins
- Dressmaker's chalk
- Upholstery foam, chair pad size
- Thick and thin variegated wool yarn, approximately 8 to 10 yards (7.3 to 9.1 m) per corner (you can needle felt one to four corners of the throw.)
- 36-gauge single felting needle
- 36-gauge multi-needle tool or felting machine (optional)
- Scissors

WHAT YOU DO

1 Spread the throw on a flat work surface. Use the tape measure and dressmaker's pins to block out the borders of your design: from 1 to 7 inches (2.5 to 17.8 cm) in from the edge, extending 24 inches (61.0 cm) in either direction from the corner. Lightly mark your scroll design within the pinned borders using dressmaker's chalk.

2 Place one corner of the throw on top of the upholstery foam. Working straight from the ball of yarn and using the 36-gauge needle, needle felt the thick tail of the yarn into one end of the design on the throw. Form a tight dot and needle felt it into the fabric to secure the yarn to the throw.

3 Continue needle felting the yarn to the design, allowing the thick and thin portions of the yarn to create a free-form pattern within the scrolling shape. To show off the colors and add interest to the design, keep the yarn slightly untwisted. If you aren't sure how it will look, tack the yarn in place with the single felting needle. If you like it, go back over it with a multi-needle tool. If you don't, gently pull it out. When you come to the end of the design, simply trim the yarn and needle felt the tail down.

4 Repeat steps 2 and 3 for the other corners, as desired. Make sure your yarn is thoroughly needle felted into the throw so it doesn't catch and pull out the yarn later.

Stained Glass Pincushion

designer
SANDIE O'NEILL

Too nice to tuck away in your sewing basket, this pincushion is as pretty as it is useful. Make it with the yarns you see here or customize the design with your favorite shades.

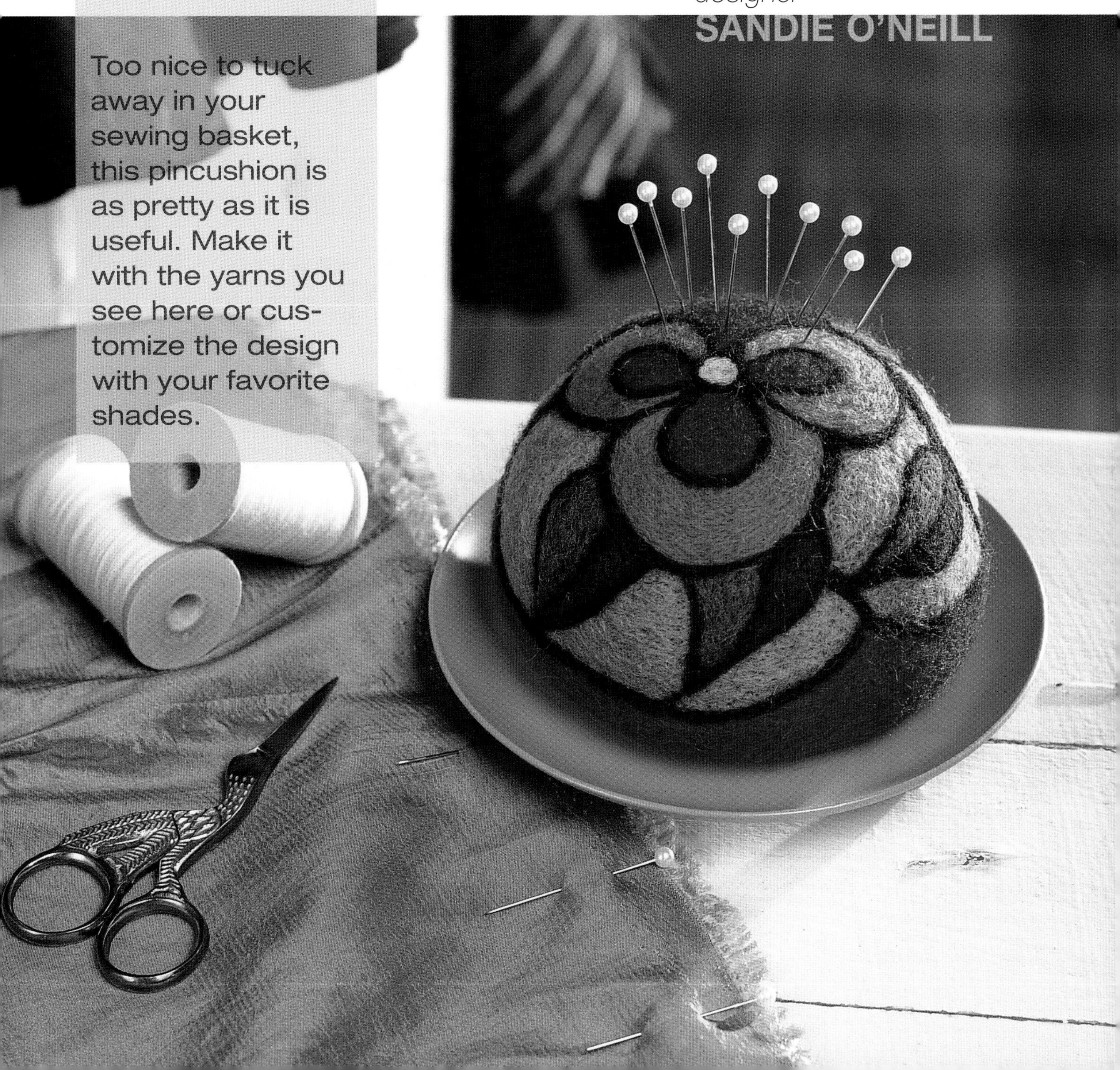

SKILL LEVEL
Beginner

FELTING METHOD USED
Dry Felting

FINISHED MEASUREMENTS
About 4 inches (10.2 cm) in diameter

WHAT YOU NEED
- 50 grams of 100% wool roving in light green
- 36-gauge triangular felting needle
- Upholstery foam
- 10 grams of 100% wool roving in lilac, purple, medium green, dark green, and black
- Small amount (about 1 gram) of 100% wool roving in bright yellow
- 38-gauge star felting needle
- 40-gauge triangular felting needle
- Pincushion base, such as a candlestick
- Multipurpose adhesive

WHAT YOU DO

1 Tear off about 11¾ inches (30.0 cm) of the light green roving and roll it into a ball, making sure the surface is smooth. Then use the 36-gauge triangular felting needle to needle felt the surface of the ball, using the upholstery foam as your work surface. Jab the ball two or three times, roll it evenly, and then jab it again. Rolling the ball in all directions helps it keep a round shape.

2 Once the ball holds its shape, wrap a bit more of the light green roving around it and needle felt the surface again. If you wrap the roving tightly, it should felt quickly. Continue adding roving and needle felting until only about 2 inches (5.1 cm) of roving remain. Put this aside in case you need it later to fix a problem. You should now have a large, squishy ball.

3 Using the 36-gauge needle, needle felt in a circular area on one side of the ball to create a flattened area that can serve as a base. Turn the piece over and needle felt across the top surface, maintaining a dome shape as you work. Work all across the surface—if you work in one area, you'll create another flat spot. Continue felting until you have a dome shape that feels firm.

4 To make the petals and leaves of the pansy (see detail photo), tear off small tufts of the roving in lilac, purple, and both shades of green. Only use what you need. Wind the tufts into flat, coiled disc shapes—you can poke them a few times with a felting needle to help them keep their coil shape—and set them aside. Using the project photo as a guide, attach a purple coil/petal to the green ball shape with the 36-gauge needle. Punch the whole surface of the petal to secure it to the green ball. If the petal is too small, tear off another sliver of roving and felt it to the perimeter of the petal to make it bigger.

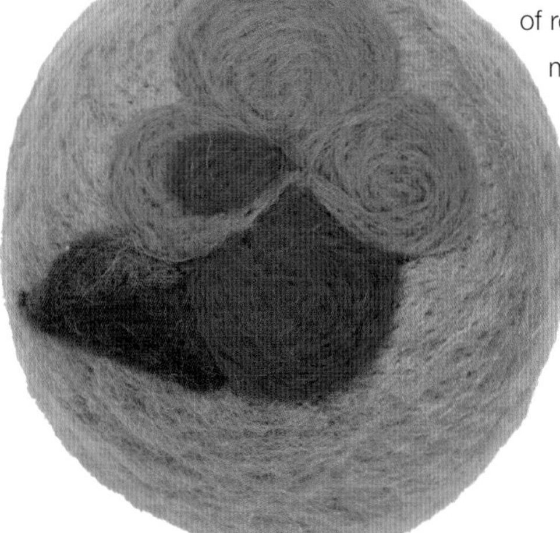

5 After you've roughly attached the first petal, continue by attaching more petals in the same manner. If you need to remove a piece, just tug it gently off the work. Then you

can move it or replace it with a new color. Once you've added all the petals, start adding the two-tone green leaves. Use the same technique you used with the petals. Finish by needle felting a small circular tuft of bright yellow roving into the center of the flower.

6 Tear off several pieces of the purple roving. Refer to the project photo to needle felt it onto the work to form a curved line around the base. Next, cover the bottom with the same color and needle felt that into place.

7 Tear off long, fine strips of the black roving. Twist the pieces between your fingers and your palms, so that you have very thin strips. Using the project photo as a guide, lay the strips around the edges of the petal/leaf designs, and use the 36-gauge needle to needle felt it. Then use the 38-gauge needle to work over the lines very carefully, needle felting along the edges so that you produce a crisp, clear line. You should also work over the rest of the pincushion periodically to ensure that you're needle felting it to the same consistency all around and that the lines don't sink into the pincushion

8 To produce a more three-dimensional piece, use the 38-gauge needle to needle felt evenly over the background surface of the pincushion. This will cause the background to recede and make the pansy look raised.

9 With the 40-gauge needle, work over the whole surface, using shallow stabs. This will smooth out the surface, eliminate any fuzziness, and make the needle holes less apparent.

10 Find a suitable base for your pincushion—candleholders make terrific stands—and glue your pincushion to the base using a multipurpose adhesive.

PATRICIA SPARK
designer

Autumn Leaves Runner

SKILL LEVEL
Advanced Beginner to Intermediate

FELTING METHOD USED
Dry Felting

FINISHED MEASUREMENTS
10 x 32 inches
(25.4 x 81.2 cm)

WHAT YOU NEED

Merino top roving, 1 ounce of each autumnal color (e.g., burnt orange, nutmeg, cinnamon, and pumpkin)

Colander, pot with lid, and stove (for preparing the roving)

Newspaper

Wool felt (can be as low as 35% wool) in green, 12 x 36 inches (30.5 x 91.5 cm)

Sink and clothes dryer (for preparing the wool felt)

Steam iron

Scissors

Leaf patterns (see page 125)

Paper and pencil

Dense foam pad, 9 x 12 x 1½ inches (22.9 x 30.5 x 3.8 cm)

Pins

2 dog brushes (optional, for carding wool)

2 40-gauge triangular felting needles

1 skein of embroidery floss and needle, in a complementary color (for edging)

Use this pretty autumn-themed piece as a seasonal table-topper or keep it out all year long for a touch of extra elegance. The leaves are needle felted from Merino top roving, which has fine fibers and produces a smooth surface.

WHAT YOU DO

To Prepare the Top Roving

1 Coil the top roving into a colander suspended over a pot of boiling water on the stove. Cover and steam the fiber for about 15 minutes, until it has plumped up and the crimp has returned. Place newspaper between the lid of the pot and the fiber. The newspaper absorbs the condensation from the lid and doesn't let any drip down onto the fiber.

2 Remove the fiber from the colander and let the steam dissipate. After a few minutes, the fiber has cooled down enough to be used.

To Prepare the Wool Felt Backing

3 Since the wool felt is quite stiff, it needs to be fulled a little more to soften its texture. Lay the piece of wool felt in a sink of hot water and gently squeeze it until the felt is saturated with water.

4 Blot the felt to remove most of the water, and then put it into the dryer on hot until it has dried. After you steam press it, you can cut it to size.

I love working with merino top roving for my needle felting because the fibers are so fine and they produce a smooth surface. But if you use the roving as it comes from the manufacturer, you can run into problems. Top roving has been combed to remove the short fibers. The remaining long fibers are straightened so that the normal curly crimp is invisible, but the curly crimp is what helps produce those nice thin layers for needle felting. So how do you get it back? Steam the fiber (see steps 1 and 2).

Pat Spark

To Make the Table Runner

5 Transfer the drawing of the leaves to the notebook paper. Cut the desired number of leaves out of the paper, retaining both the positive and the negative shapes (the paper that has the cut-out shape of the leaf). You'll use the positive shapes to help position the leaves (see detail photo for placement). You'll use the negative shapes as the stencil to create the leaf shapes.

6 Lay the wool felt backing on the foam pad. Arrange the leaves and pin them down. I put the same design on both ends, but you can do whatever you'd like. Choose one leaf and place its negative shape into position around it. Pin down the negative and remove the positive leaf template.

7 To blend the various colored roving to fill in the shapes, pull off a little of one color and a bit of another color. Use your fingers to blend the two colors together. If you know how to card (see Blending Different Colors of Wool Together on page 14), you could use dog brushes to blend the wool. You don't need large hand cards because the amounts are so small.

8 After blending, crisscross the wool pieces in the shape you're filling so they extend a little beyond the edge of the stencil. Needle felt around the contour of the stencil with the triangular felting needle. You don't need to push the blade all the way down to the hilt; you can get enough tangled attachments by just using a few of the needle's barbs.

9 After you've needle felted the outline, fold the extended fiber into the center and needle felt it down, from the edge toward the center of the shape. Add more fiber (in small chunks) to get better coverage, if needed. Otherwise, it might get too bulky.

10 After you've completed the leaf, remove the stencil. Pick another leaf, and pin down its negative stencil, removing the positive leaf template. Needle felt this leaf like you did the first. Complete all the leaves on both ends of the runner in this manner.

11 Blend some fiber and draw it out into a loosely twisted yarn. Needle felt this yarn down to create the stems on the leaves. Notice that the stems curve slightly to create a sense of movement with the leaves.

12 Turn the table runner over and needle felt it a little from the back.

13 Then turn it back to the front and use just the ends of the needles to punch the surface of the felt to tighten it up. If you hold two needles together in your hand and gently jab with just the tips, you will tighten the felt surface without pushing the colored fiber out the back of the table runner.

14 When you've completed needle felting, finish off the edge of the runner with three strands of embroidery floss (or other desired yarn or thread), worked in a blanket stitch (see Using Embroidery Stitches on page 21). Steam press and enjoy!

TIP

I usually use two felting needles at the same time, but you can use a single needle if you want.

Pat Spark

This project was completed with:

Ashland Bay Brand merino top roving in Burnt Orange, Nutmeg, Cinnabar, and Pumpkin

National Nonwovens WoolFelt (35% wool/65% rayon) in #0730 Moss

DMC Embroidery floss #221 Shell Pink

Projects to Wear

Felt is not only smooth and soft, it's also warm and cozy. Drape yourself and your loved ones with the creative garments described in this chapter. Whether you're making a scarf from scratch (actually, you use an old sweater) or embellishing an existing vest, sweater, or jacket, the end result will be a unique piece of clothing you'll be proud to own and wear.

BETZ WHITE
designer

Chili Today, Hot Tamale Scarf and Hat

THE SCARF

SKILL LEVEL
Intermediate

FELTING METHOD USED
Dry Felting

FINISHED MEASUREMENTS
Approximately 6 x 72 inches (15.2 x 182.8 cm)

WHAT YOU NEED
2 secondhand cashmere sweaters, one red and one gold

Washing machine and dryer

Scissors

Steam iron

Rotary cutter and mat

Metal-edge ruler

Sewing machine

Disappearing ink marker

Needle-felting mat

Red and orange roving

Multi-needle tool with 36-gauge needles

Press cloth

Pins

Foam mat

36-gauge single felting needle

Red and orange curly mohair locks

Needle and thread

Just what you need to survive until Spring. Fringed in red and flaming orange mohair, this bright scarf and hat set will keep you toasty warm all winter long. The scarf is made from recycled sweaters that are wet felted, cut into pieces, and sewn together.

WHAT YOU DO TO MAKE THE SCARF

1 Wash both sweaters in a washing machine with hot water. Dry on low. The cashmere will not felt, but it will shrink, soften, and get nice and fuzzy.

2 Cut the sweaters apart with the scissors. Steam press out any wrinkles using an iron on the wrong side of the fabric.

3 Using the rotary cutter and the ruler, cut four rectangles from the first sweater measuring 6 x 18 inches (15.2 x 45.7 cm), or whatever dimensions you desire for your scarf. Cut the longest dimension with the grain. Repeat with the second sweater.

4 With the sewing machine, straight stitch together the short ends of rectangles from the red sweater, forming one side of the scarf. Repeat for the gold rectangles.

5 Use the disappearing ink marker to draw flame shapes at both ends of the gold side of the scarf.

6 Lay one end of the scarf onto the needle-felting mat. Place wisps of red roving onto the scarf, following the flame shapes. Needle felt them into place with the multi-needle tool.

THE HAT

SKILL LEVEL
Beginner

FELTING METHOD USED
Dry Felting

FINISHED MEASUREMENTS
Your Hat Size

WHAT YOU NEED
Knit hat with cuff, red or orange

Foam mat

36-gauge single felting needle

Red and orange curly mohair locks

7 Overlap the felted area with a second layer of roving wisps, using orange in more flame shapes. Needle felt them into place. Trim the overhanging roving across the bottom edge. Repeat for the other end of the gold side of the scarf.

8 Cover the scarf with the press cloth and steam press it to set the fibers.

9 Place the right sides together, red to gold, and pin them together. Straight stitch across the scarf ends only.

10 Spread open one end seam and place the back side onto the foam mat. With the 36-gauge single felting needle, attach the curly mohair locks by poking the middle of the lock directly into the seam at the bottom of the flames. Continue across the seam, creating curly "fringe." Repeat for the other end of the scarf.

11 Placing right sides together, red to gold, pin the long edges of the scarf together. Straight stitch around the entire scarf, leaving a 5-inch (12.7 cm) opening for turning the work. (Take care not to catch any of the fringe in the seams as you stitch.)

12 Clip the corners and turn the scarf right side out. Cover with the press cloth and steam.

13 Hand stitch the opening closed with the needle and thread.

WHAT YOU DO TO MAKE THE HAT

1 Use a handknit or purchased hat with a cuff. Turn the hat inside out and place the cuff on the foam mat, with the right side of the cuff facing you.

2 With the 36-gauge needle, attach the curly mohair locks by poking the middle of the lock into the edge of the cuff.

3 Continue across the edge, creating a curly "fringe."

Old World Cuffs and Collar

designer
LISA CRUSE

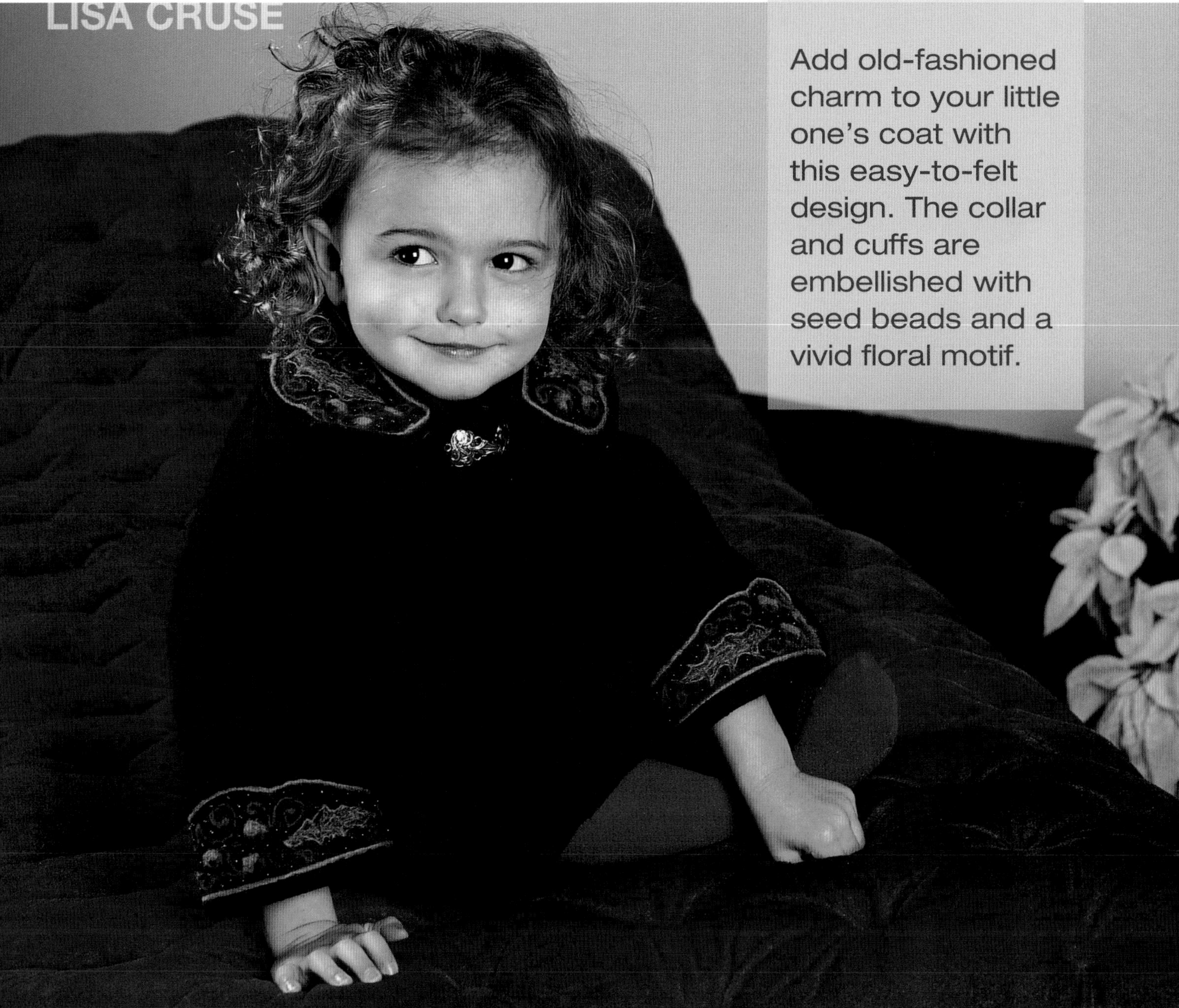

Add old-fashioned charm to your little one's coat with this easy-to-felt design. The collar and cuffs are embellished with seed beads and a vivid floral motif.

SKILL LEVEL
Intermediate

FELTING METHOD USED
Dry Felting

FINISHED MEASUREMENTS
Collar: Approximately 3 x 8¼ inches (7.6 x 20.3 cm)

Cuffs: Each approximately 2¾ x 11 inches (7.0 x 27.9 cm)

WHAT YOU NEED

Tape measure

Child's black coat, 12-month size

Pattern (see page 125)

Dressmaker's chalk

2 squares of wool or wool-blend felt, each 9 x 12 inches (22.9 x 30.5 cm), in the same desired color

Scissors

36-gauge felting needle

Scraps of wool yarn in several shades of green, two shades of berry red, rust, orange, and black

Upholstery foam

Glass seed beads, size 11, dark brown

Beading needle

Beading thread

Pins

WHAT YOU DO

1 Lay the coat flat. With the tape measure, measure the circumference of one of the cuffs and adjust the cuff pattern dimensions to fit the measurement. Then measure the coat collar and adjust the collar pattern dimensions accordingly. (The example shows a felt upper collar that completely covers the coat collar; make yours as large or as small as desired.)

2 Enlarge and photocopy the patterns on page 125. Trace the patterns onto one of the felt squares, marking any changes in size. Then cut the collar and two cuffs out of the felt with the scissors.

3 To needle felt the collar and cuffs, use the 36-gauge needle and the black wool yarn. Use the upholstery foam as your work surface. Needle felt an outline with the black wool yarn, ⅛ inch (3 mm) in from the cut edges. Then needle felt a line of rust wool adjacent to and inside the outline of black wool (see detail photo).

4 Needle felt the leaves by working an outline with wool in a medium green. Then fill in the outline with wool in different tones of green. To make a vein down the

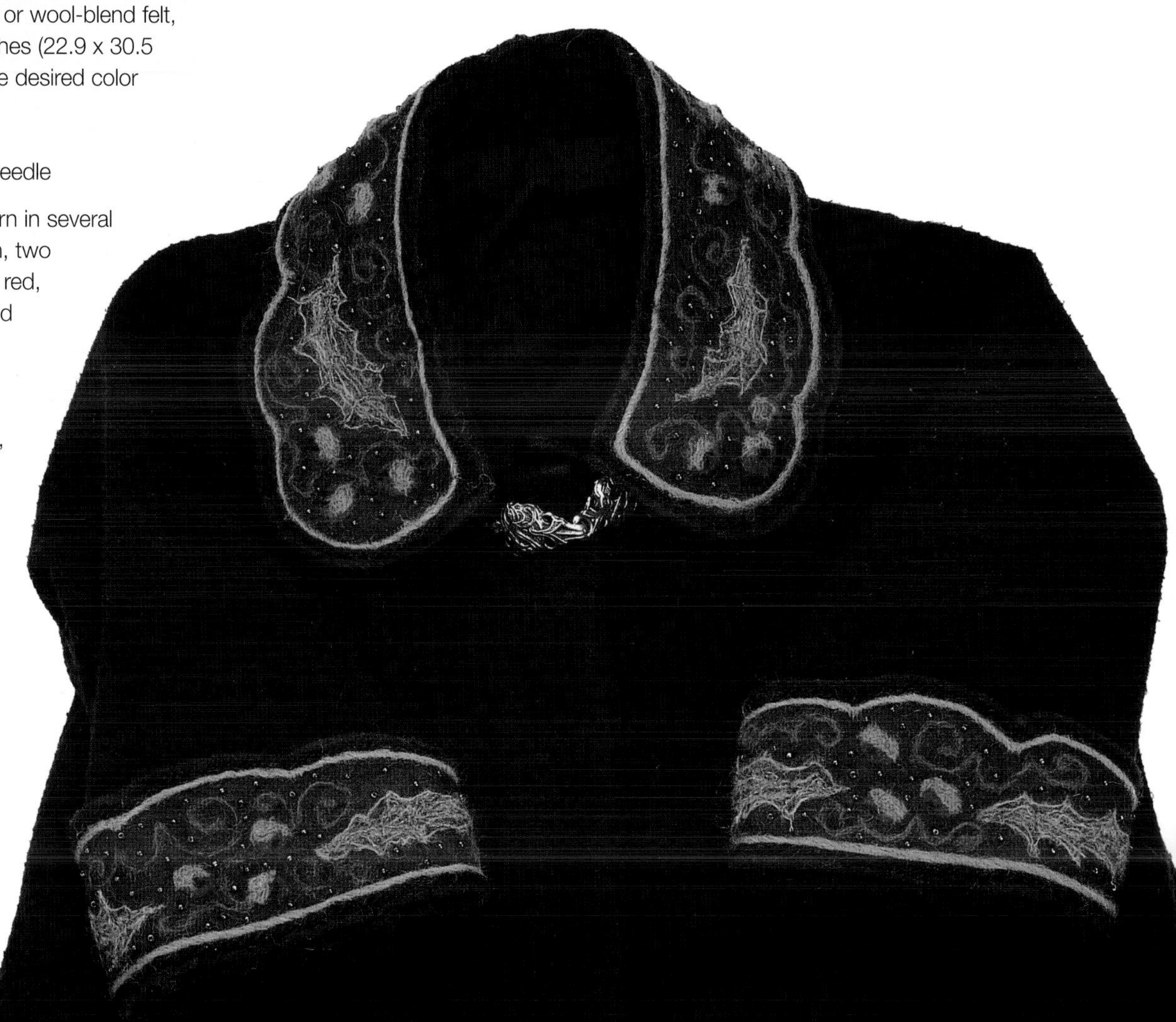

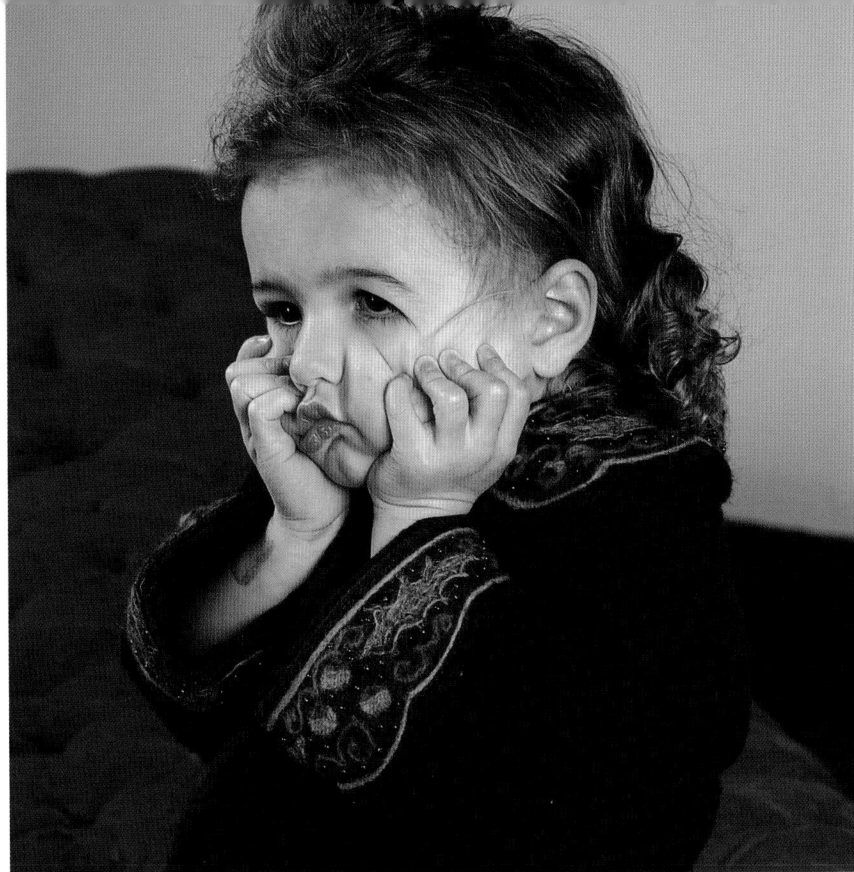

center of the leaf, use wool in a contrasting shade of green. You should needle felt two leaves on each cuff and one leaf on each section of the collar (See detail photo).

5 To needle felt one berry, use the darkest shade of berry red wool, filling in the whole berry shape with the wool. Use the rust wool to give the berry contour, and the orange wool to create highlights. Then use the black wool to needle felt a spot of black at the bottom end of the berry. You should needle felt three berries on each cuff and seven berries on each section of the collar (see detail photo).

6 Split the yarn into single plies and embellish the design with swirls done in a single fine ply of rust wool (see detail photo).

7 Using the beading needle and thread, randomly stitch the beads in and around the needle-felted design (see detail photo).

8 Pin the collar in place and stitch invisibly between the felting lines at the neck edge, joining the needle felted collar to the fold of the coat collar. Wherever possible, invisibly tack stitch the upper collar to the under collar to secure the sides and outer edges.

9 Pin the cuffs into place, making sure that the lower edges are lined up with the edges of the sleeves. Stitch invisibly and securely to join the ends at the seam line and between the needle felted lines around the edges.

TIP

When you work the felting designs, you should reverse the patterns for the left and right sides.

Lisa Cruse

designer

LK LUDWIG

Shibori Felted Scarves

SKILL LEVEL
Beginner

FELTING METHODS USED
Dry Felting and Wet Felting

FINISHED MEASUREMENTS
Approximately 30 to 36 inches (76.2 to 91.5 cm)

WHAT YOU NEED

Cutting mat

Rotary cutter

Large wool sweater

Thread to match the sweater

Sewing machine

Buttons, bingo chips, game pieces, marbles, small stones, and slices of cork (to create bobbles)

Small rubber bands (orthodontic bands work very well) or cotton string

Lingerie laundry bag

Washing machine

Upholstery foam

Small amounts of 100% wool yarn, in desired colors, for embellishment

38-gauge multi-needle felting tool

Sharp scissors

Machine-felted sweater scraps for embellishment (from different sweaters)

Steam iron

Turning an old wool sweater into one of these sophisticated scarves is a snap. You'll use wet and dry felting techniques on the fabric, and then add special embellishments—buttons, stones, even bingo chips (use your imagination!)—as a finishing touch.

WHAT YOU DO

1 Using the rotary cutter and cutting mat, cut the sweater according to diagram A. Remove the waistband, if present. Test felt the upper portion as indicated in the diagram (see Fulling Woven or Knit Wool Yardage on page 20).

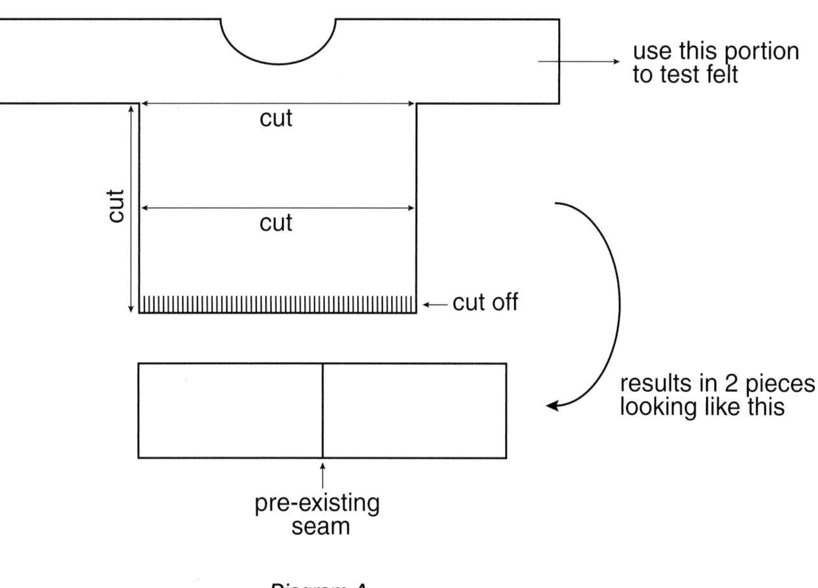

Diagram A

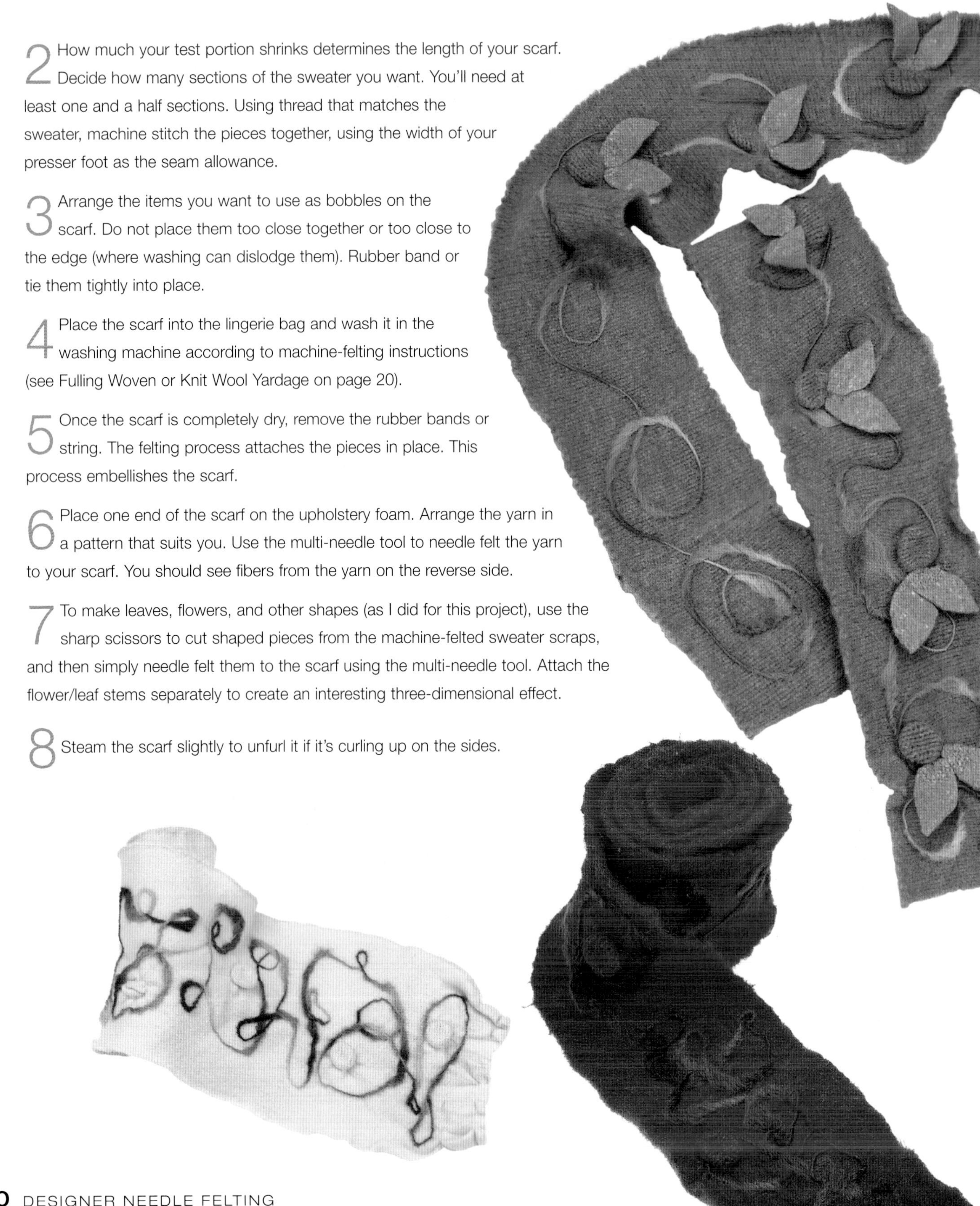

2 How much your test portion shrinks determines the length of your scarf. Decide how many sections of the sweater you want. You'll need at least one and a half sections. Using thread that matches the sweater, machine stitch the pieces together, using the width of your presser foot as the seam allowance.

3 Arrange the items you want to use as bobbles on the scarf. Do not place them too close together or too close to the edge (where washing can dislodge them). Rubber band or tie them tightly into place.

4 Place the scarf into the lingerie bag and wash it in the washing machine according to machine-felting instructions (see Fulling Woven or Knit Wool Yardage on page 20).

5 Once the scarf is completely dry, remove the rubber bands or string. The felting process attaches the pieces in place. This process embellishes the scarf.

6 Place one end of the scarf on the upholstery foam. Arrange the yarn in a pattern that suits you. Use the multi-needle tool to needle felt the yarn to your scarf. You should see fibers from the yarn on the reverse side.

7 To make leaves, flowers, and other shapes (as I did for this project), use the sharp scissors to cut shaped pieces from the machine-felted sweater scraps, and then simply needle felt them to the scarf using the multi-needle tool. Attach the flower/leaf stems separately to create an interesting three-dimensional effect.

8 Steam the scarf slightly to unfurl it if it's curling up on the sides.

Adorned Denim Vest

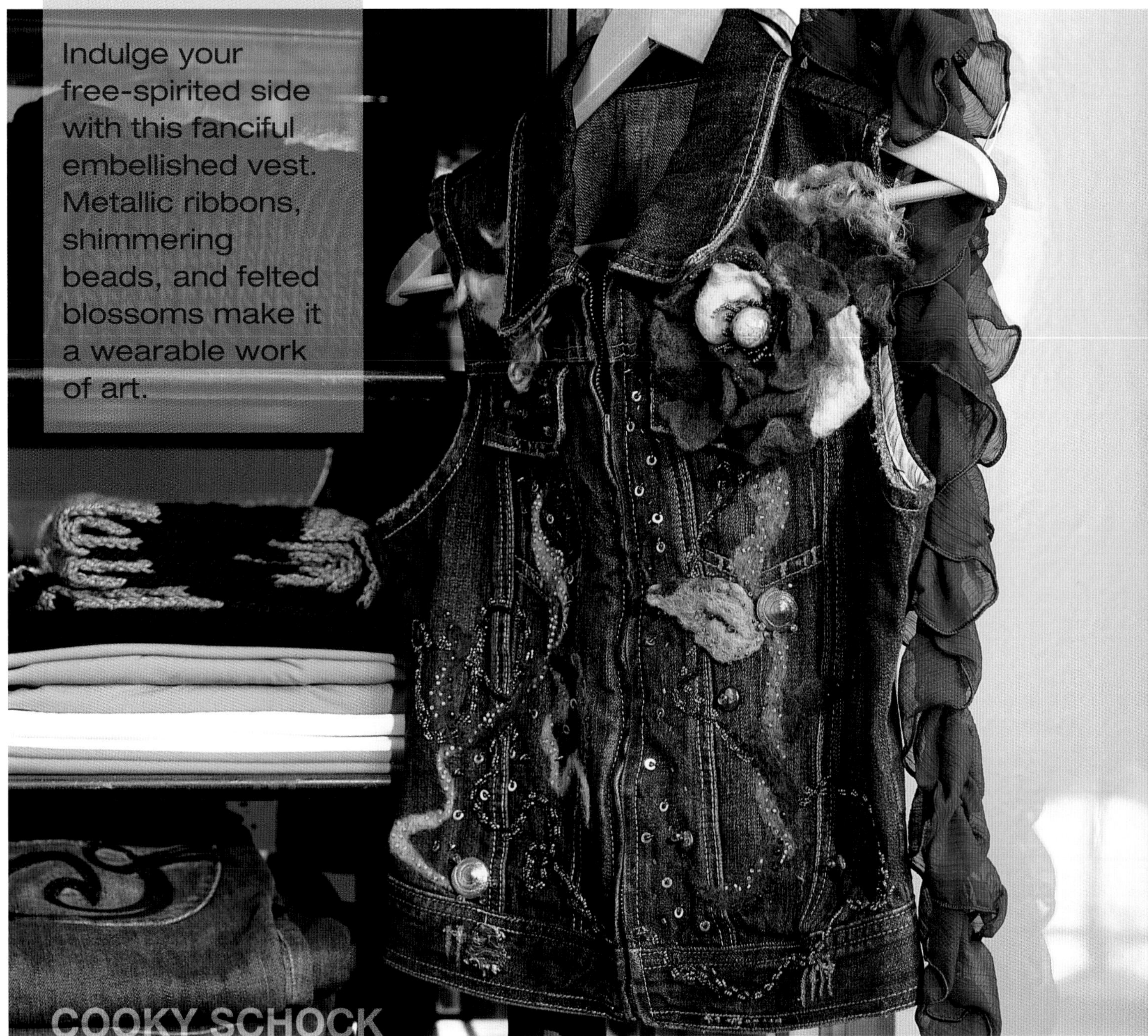

Indulge your free-spirited side with this fanciful embellished vest. Metallic ribbons, shimmering beads, and felted blossoms make it a wearable work of art.

COOKY SCHOCK

designer

SKILL LEVEL
Beginner

FELTING METHODS USED
Dry Felting and Wet Felting

FINISHED MEASUREMENTS
Size of chosen garment

WHAT YOU NEED
Wool roving in complementary colors, enough to complete your design

Bamboo mat or bubble wrap, about placemat size (the wet-felting work surface)

Hot water

Liquid soap

Scissors

Cold water, 4 cups

White vinegar, ⅛ cup

4 thick towels

Sewing thread in any color or rubber band

Flat metallic ribbon, size and length dependent on size of garment and design

Garment of choice (denim should be pre-washed to remove sizing or stiffness)

38-gauge felting needle

Upholstery foam, 10 inches (25.4 cm) square, 2 inches (5.1 cm) thick

Spray bottle with room-temperature water

Steam iron

Variety of beads

Beading needles and beading thread to match wool

Embroidery thread and needle (optional)

WHAT YOU DO

To Make the Wet-Felted Flower

1 Layer the wool fibers in three layers, as you would to make a wet-felted sheet of wool (see Wet Felting on page 19). Place the first layer horizontally, the second vertically, and the last horizontally. Create square and rectangular shapes in various sizes, from 3 x 3 inches (7.5 x 7.5 cm) to 6 x 9 inches (15.2 x 22.9 cm).

2 One at a time, place them on your wet-felting work surface.

3 Sprinkle the fiber sandwich with hot water, pat the water into the fiber, and continue sprinkling water until the fiber is thoroughly wet. Rub soap on your hands and gently rub the soap into the fiber. Continue until the piece is wet and soapy, and the fibers have begun to mesh together. Then roll the piece sushi-style, in both directions, to agitate the fibers together.

4 Before the piece is completely felted, use scissors to cut petals into the fiber. Cut the petals irregularly to give them an organic look. Then roll the piece up again and agitate it until the fibers are completely felted.

5 Rinse the piece in cold water and vinegar until all the soapsuds are gone. Then roll it in a thick, clean towel to remove as much water as possible.

6 Repeat steps 3 through 5 with the other pieces (the square and rectangular "sandwiches" you created).

7 Layer and shape the pieces so that they form a flower. Once you're satisfied with the shape, tie the piece with thread or place a rubber band around it, and let it dry naturally.

TIP

Be careful when needle felting over seams—you can easily break a needle because of the thickness of the seams.

Cooky Schock

To Embellish the Surface

8 Position the flat metallic ribbon on the garment in a way that appeals to you, and then tack it in place with the sewing thread. To conceal the ribbon ends, tuck them underneath the ribbon or cover them with needle felting using the 38-gauge felting needle (see detail photo).

9 Lay the garment right side up on the piece of foam. Separate a small amount of wool roving, and then arrange it into simple geometric shapes, such as swirls or lines.

10 Using the 38-gauge needle, felt the roving to the garment. Lift the piece up frequently to avoid felting it to the foam. Some fibers will push through to the wrong side, but most of them will remain on the front surface. Try building up areas by adding more fiber, and leaving other areas wispy (less felted). This will create texture and give the piece a more interesting surface.

11 After you're done needle felting, spray the front and back surfaces of the piece with water, so that it's barely damp. Fold a towel up and lay the garment face down on it. With the steam iron set on wool, steam and lightly press the wrong side of the garment. This helps felt the fibers together. Then turn the garment over and lightly steam the front side, but don't press down. This helps fluff the fibers. Now hang the garment and let it dry.

To Finish the Piece

12 Add color and interest to your piece with beads. Don't be afraid of color-the beads will settle down into the felt and become subtle. If desired, add embroidery stitches for embellishment—the knots can be hidden in the fibers. Have fun with this part of the project, but don't overwhelm or obscure the wonderful texture you created with the needle felting.

This project was completed with:

Ozark Handspun 100% wool roving, in a variety of complementary colors

Harrisville Designs 100% wool roving, in a variety of complementary colors

Muench Yarns Verikeri, a flat metallic ribbon yarn

designer

PAULA SCAFFIDI

Elegance Personified Evening Sweater

SKILL LEVEL
Beginner

FELTING METHOD USED
Dry Felting

FINISHED MEASUREMENTS
The size of the sweater

WHAT YOU NEED

Wool pullover sweater, in a solid color (see step 1)

Scissors

Tape measure

Pins

Chalk marker

6 to 8 yards (5.5 to 7.3 m) roving, in assorted colors

38-gauge needle-felting machine and spare needles

Dress form or padded hanger

5 yards (4.5 m) yarn of at least 75% wool content

Rejuvenate a sweater with the feeling of a favorite place. Your memories influence your choice of fibers, colors, and patterns. Transform an ordinary garment into something extraordinary while exploring the creative potential of needle felting.

WHAT YOU DO

1 Find a solid-color pullover sweater that fits or is slightly oversized. A lightweight, thin sweater will drape nicely even after adding layers of roving. Lambswool or merino wool sweaters work especially well.

2 With the scissors, remove all the tags and labels from the sweater. Cut off any ribbing at the cuffs, bottom edge, and neck. If it has a polo, crew, or ribbed collar, cut that off completely as well. If the sweater is old, gently hand wash it in cool water. Blot out the excess water by rolling the sweater in a towel. Then reshape it and lay it flat to dry.

3 Lay the sweater flat and measure to find the center of the front. Mark the centerline with the pins or chalk, and then cut it open. Now try the sweater on as a cardigan. Cut off a little at a time around the neck and front, trying the sweater on each time you trim. Gradually reshape the sweater until it hangs gracefully on the body. If you trim the front width narrower than the back, you can add the missing width later when you create the felt trim for the opening.

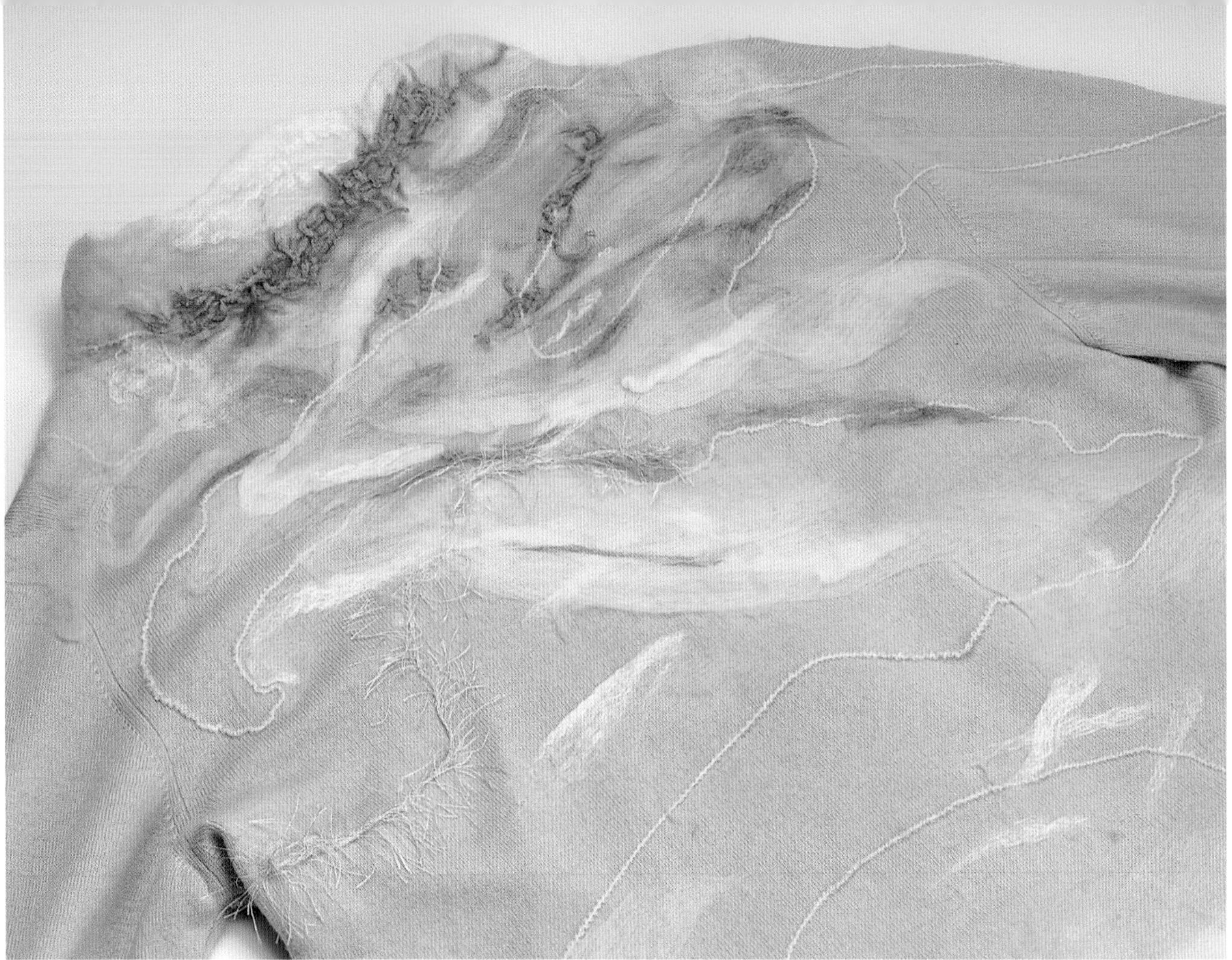

4 To seal the knit edges you've cut, you'll apply roving over the edges in three layers, needle felting each layer before proceeding to the next. Lay the first layer, made up of wisps of roving on top along the sweater's edges, overlapping the cut edge by 1 to 2 inches (2.5 to 5.1 cm). Place the roving at about a 45° angle and needle felt them into the base of the sweater. Continue in this manner until you have worked all the way around the center opening, neck area, and bottom edge. At the corners, rotate the direction of the roving.

5 Turn the sweater inside side out. Apply the second layer of roving in the opposite direction of the first layer (as if the roving repeatedly forms an X over the last layer). Needle felt the layer onto the sweater.

6 For the third and final layer, turn the sweater right side out again, and repeat step 4, laying the roving in the same direction. Use delicate or heavier roving in this layer, depending on how much drape you want along the finished sweater's edge.

7 Repeat the process (all three layers) for the cuffs. Use the free-arm option on your needle-felting machine.

TIP

You can find old sweaters in thrift stores on the menswear rack. You can reverse needle felt any wool sweater to visually blend the base color into the roving colors. This technique can also help secure a less felt-able yarn. Test the yarn by felting a couple of inches onto the ribbing, and then evaluate whether or not it securely felts into place.

Paula Scaffidi

8 The edges still probably look a bit wild and wooly. Shape them however you wish with the scissors—make them fringy, funky, or formal. The shapes you cut might suggest clouds, grasses, rolling hills, or piles of leaves. Place the sweater on a dress form or hanger, step back, and check it out. Try it on and look in the mirror. You can build the collar as high as you want. Let the front opening roll a bit or try overlapping the edges as much as you prefer. If you accidentally cut off something you wish you hadn't, reattach it or build the edge back up with more roving.

9 Place the sweater back on the dress form/hanger and lay the yarn on the sweater, playing with different arrangements. Don't cut the yarn yet—just arrange it and pin it into place. Your design goal is to add some slimming, graceful lines—diagonal, wavy, or otherwise—to the sweater. As you're pinning, try to conjure a sense of place.

10 Try on the sweater, evaluating where you placed the yarn. Adjust it to please your eye. Use the chalk marker to clearly mark the entire path of the yarn. Then remove the yarn. Since the yarn will shrink as you felt it into place, feed as much yarn as the needles will take while working your way around the chalk lines. Use little zigzag or circular motions to felt the yarn all the way through to the back.

COLOR PALETTE DESIGN TIPS

Does the color of the sweater remind you of anything? Mine made me think of the inside of seashells. You can use a memory of a favorite place to come up with additional colors. Or gather a few colors of roving that complement the color of your sweater and see what the combination brings to mind.

Paula Scaffidi

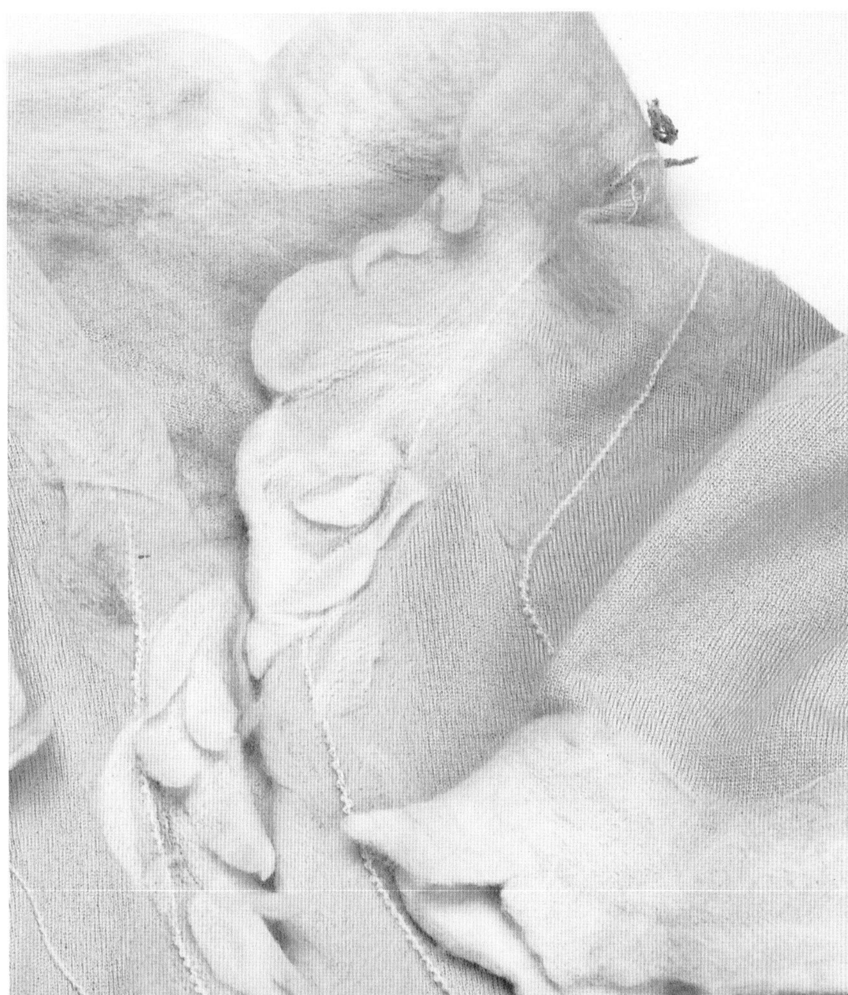

11 If your yarn is not felting well, try reverse needle felting. Turn the sweater over so the yarn is facing the machine's throat plate and needle felt the piece again. Reverse needle felting also softens any line or shape by blurring it slightly. Additionally, reverse felting blends the sweater color into applied roving for harmony.

Hint: Two other ways to solve felting problems are twisting some roving around your yarn or twirling your yarn with a pure wool yarn.

12 Prepare to embellish the sweater by dividing the back into horizontal thirds, not counting the collar or bottom edge. Use the pins or chalk to mark the divisions. You'll cover about 80% of the top third with roving, about 40% of the midsection, and 15% of the bottom third. Use a color combination that conjures up a feeling of the place you are recalling. Select some colors that are similar and some that offer contrast. You can blend in even a starkly contrasting color with the direct application techniques we'll use. The sweater color will gradually emerge from the heavily felted top area to the lightly felted lower area.

13 Direct application techniques require no pre-felting. Simply place non-felted materials directly onto the sweater and felt into place. The wisps of roving will shrink toward the felting needles. Let it. You can always apply more roving to cover the area. Allowing the roving to shrink prevents the base material from puckering. When designing, place the sweater on the dress form or lay it out flat on a table. Arrange some wisps of roving. If it looks good, felt it down. Continue to design and needle felt as you go, bit by bit.

14 Creating soft, gradual blends adds beauty and harmony to your design. One way to blend colors is to apply one delicate wisp of roving after another, layer by layer, felting in between as you go. A second technique is to hand blend transitional colors by stacking two different colors, gently pulling and restacking repeatedly. After 10 to 20 pulls, a new color emerges. A third way is to reverse needle felt (see step 11).

TIP

Your roving should be clean of all foreign matter and spent dye molecules. If you're unsure of the quality of your roving, pre-wash it by hand in cool water without agitating it (leaving it gently rolled), rinse it well, roll it in a towel, and then hang or lay it flat to dry.

Paula Scaffidi

Oooh la la Berets

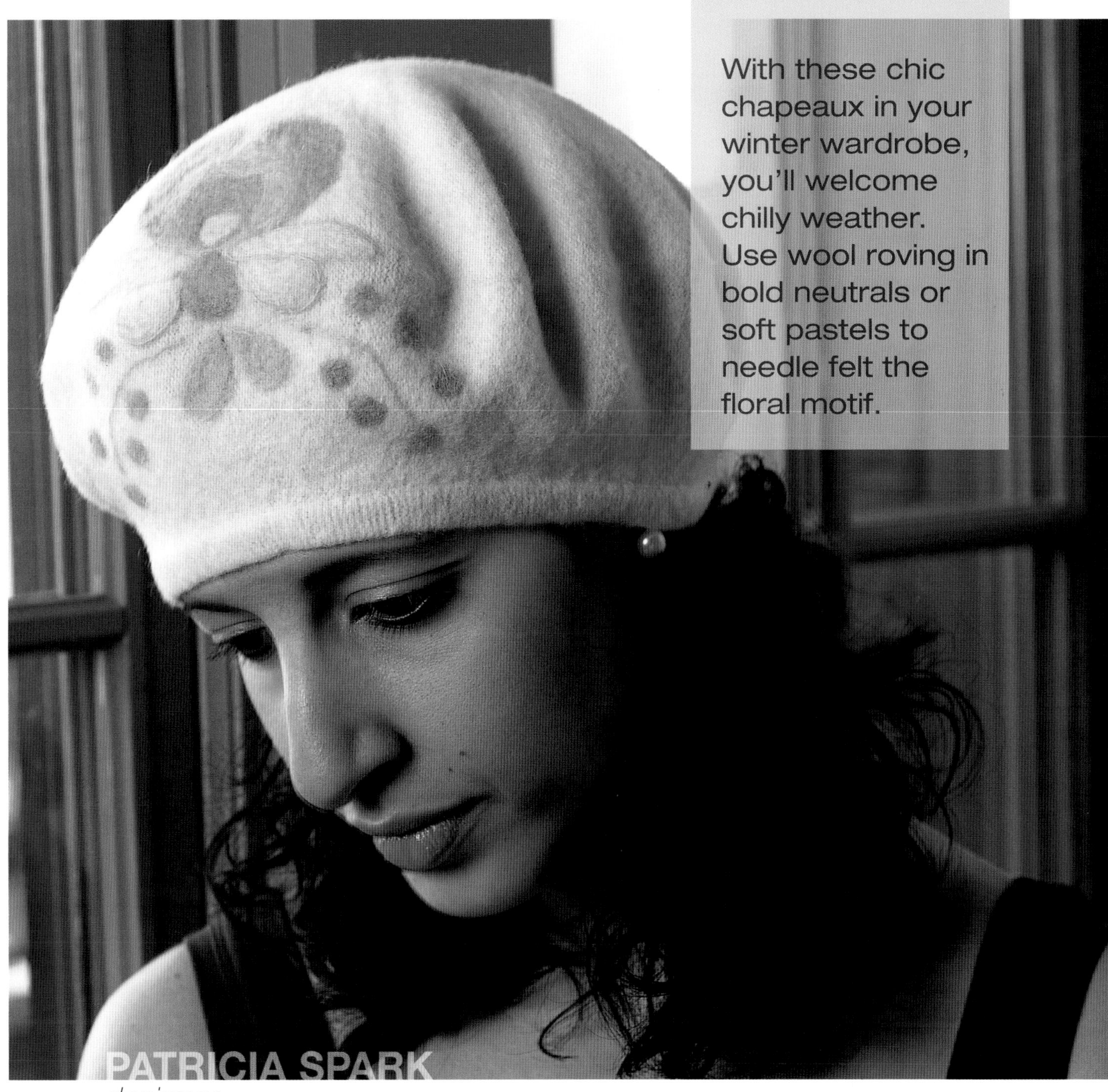

With these chic chapeaux in your winter wardrobe, you'll welcome chilly weather. Use wool roving in bold neutrals or soft pastels to needle felt the floral motif.

PATRICIA SPARK
designer

SKILL LEVEL

Advanced Beginner to Intermediate

FELTING METHODS USED

Beret One: Dry Felting and Wet Felting

Beret Two: Dry Felting

FINISHED MEASUREMENTS

Medium Beret (about an 11-inch [27.9-cm] circumference)

WHAT YOU NEED

Merino wool top roving, 1 ounce of each color listed below:

Beret One: buff, peach, vanilla, and turquoise green

Beret Two: pewter, white, dark chocolate, and mocha

Colander, pot with lid, and stove (for preparing the roving)

Newspaper

Flower motif (see page 125)

2 commercially made knit-felt berets

Pencil

Upholstery foam pad, 4 x 6 x 1½ inches (10.2 x 15.2 x 3.8 cm)

Two 40-gauge triangular felting needles

Beret 2

WHAT YOU DO

Note: If you use roving as it comes from the manufacturer, you can have problems. To return its normal curly crimp, steam the fiber (see steps 1 and 2).

1 Coil the top roving into a colander suspended over a pot of boiling water on the stove. Place newspaper between the lid of the pot and the fiber. The newspaper absorbs the condensation from the lid and doesn't let any drip down onto the fiber. Cover and steam the fiber for about 15 minutes, until it has plumped up and the crimp has returned.

2 Remove the fiber from the colander and let the steam dissipate. After a few minutes, the fiber will have cooled down enough to use.

3 Transfer the drawing of the flower motif to the beret. See the detail photo for placement. I used a sharp pencil and drew the motif freehand on the beret, but you could use some other transfer method.

4 Lay the beret open on the foam pad. Break up the roving for the center of the flower into ½- to ⅝-inch (1.3 to 1.6 cm) pieces. Start with the inside shapes and then work your way to the outside shapes. Lay the roving on the shape you're filling so it extends beyond the edge a little. Crisscross the pieces for better coverage.

5 Needle felt around the outside of the shape with the 40-gauge triangular needles. Don't push the needles all the way down to the hilt, which can push the majority of the fiber out the back of the beret. You can get enough tangled attachments by just using a few of the needle's barbs.

6 After you've needle felted the outline, fold the extended fiber into the center and needle felt it down, from the border toward the center of the shape. If needed, add more fiber to get better coverage. Break it into small pieces so it's not too bulky.

7 Continue to follow the color pattern and fill in the rest of the shapes.

8 Turn the piece over and needle felt a little from the back side.

9 Turn the beret back to the front side and use just the ends of both needles to punch the surface of the felt to tighten it up. The needle tip has one barb in it; if you hold two needles together in your hand and gently jab with just the tips, you'll tighten the felt surface without causing the colored fiber to push out the back of the beret.

10 You can wet felt the finished product, if you wish. (See Wet Felting on page 20.) I decided to wet felt Beret One as an experiment, but the beret shrank a little and became less flexible. Whether to wet felt or not is a decision you should make carefully.

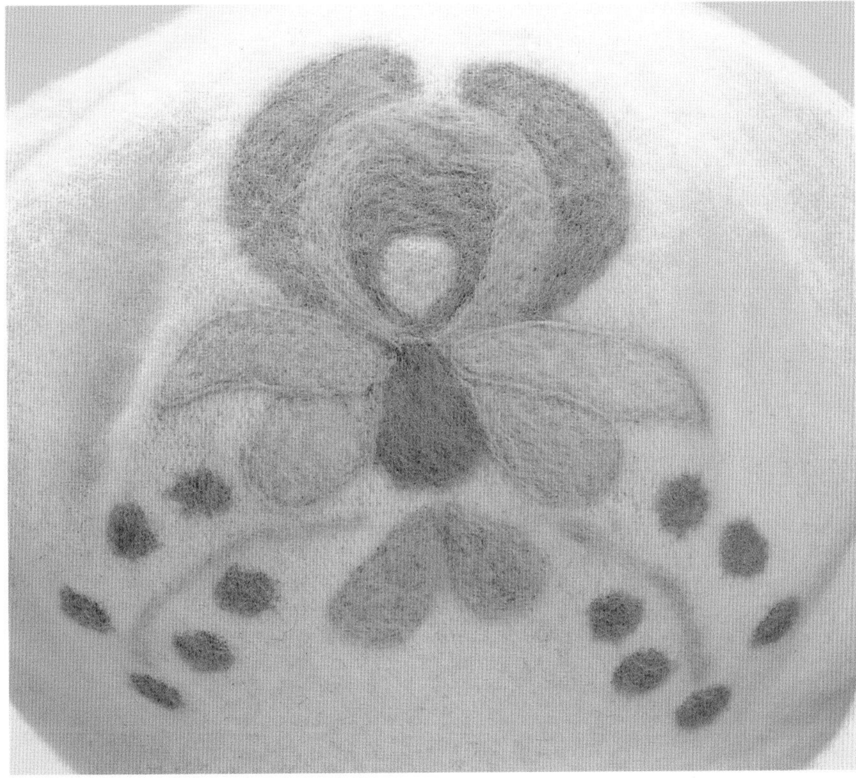

Beret 1

This project was completed with:

Ashland Bay Brand top roving

Accessories

Needle felting isn't used just for making clothes these days. You can needle felt bags, baubles, and bangles—everything a needle-felting gal could want to accessorize her outfit. Jewelry too! The projects on the following pages will teach you how to needle felt three-dimensional shapes to create earrings, necklaces, and pins. You can even learn how to make a case for eyeglasses that's too pretty to pack in your purse.

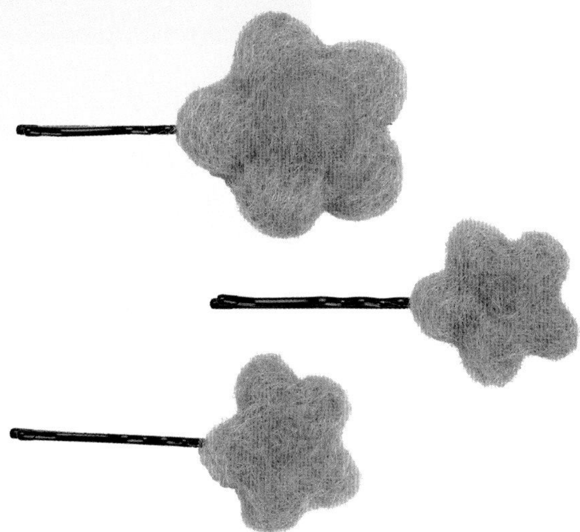

designer

LINDSAY OBERMEYER

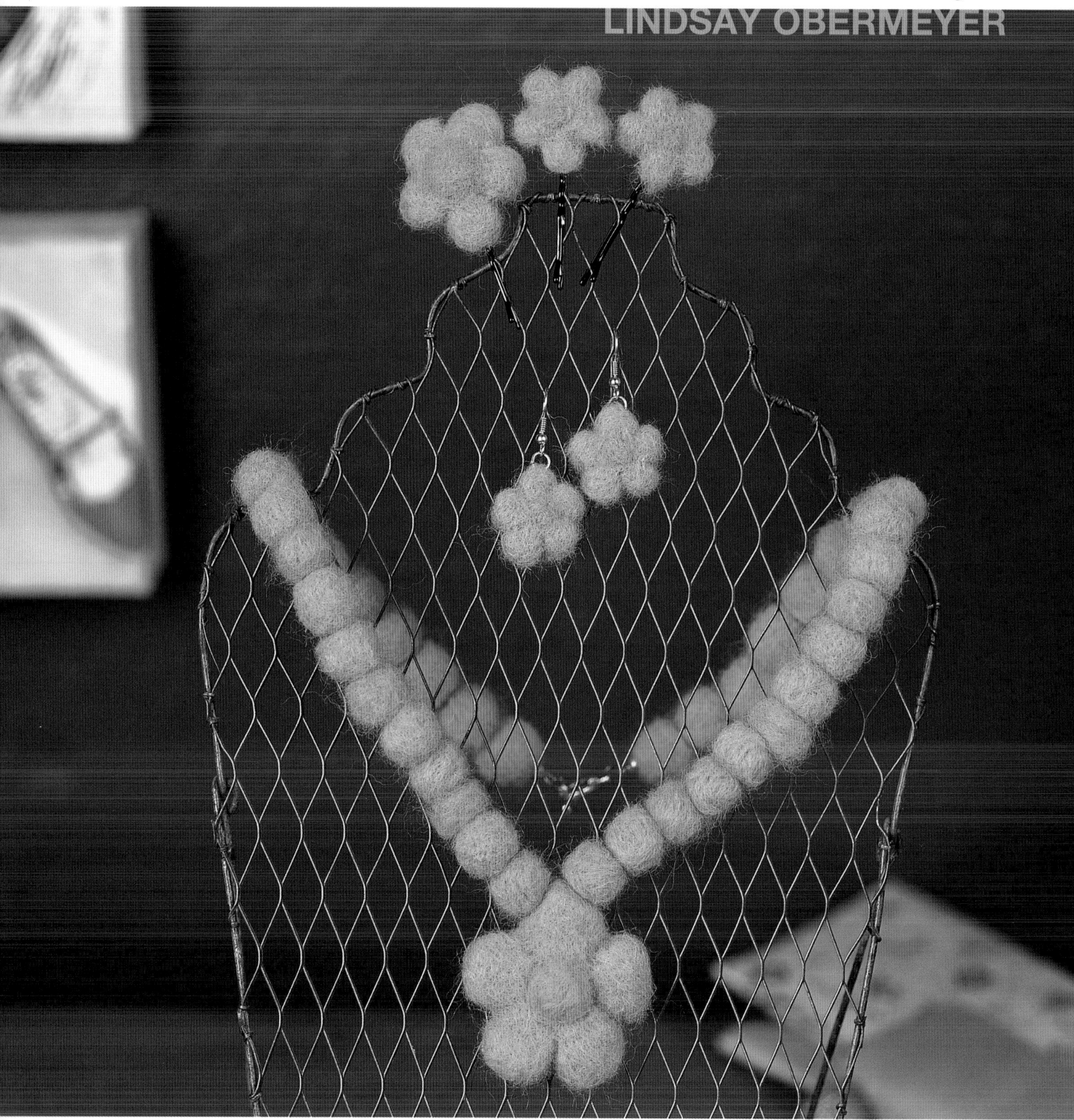

Gerber Daisy Jewelry

GERBER DAISY BOBBY PINS

SKILL LEVEL
Beginner

FELTING METHOD USED
Dry Felting

FINISHED MEASUREMENTS
Big charm: 1¼ inches (3.2 cm)

Small charm: ¾ inch (1.9 cm)

WHAT YOU NEED
Scissors

12 inches (30.5 cm) of wool roving in pink

Upholstery foam, 3 inches (7.6 cm) thick

40-gauge felting needle

12 inches (30.5 cm) of wool roving in light orange

38-gauge star felting needle

Awl

2 bobby pins

Wool roving in cheery shades of pink and orange make this jewelry ensemble blossom. The classic flower shape is simple to needle felt.

WHAT YOU DO TO MAKE THE BOBBY PINS

To Make the Large/Small Charm

1 With the scissors, cut a 4-inch (10.2 cm) piece of the pink roving for the large charm or a 3-inch (7.6 cm) piece for the small charm. Split the piece in half and shape it into a rough square by positioning half the roving vertically and the other half horizontally.

2 Place the wool onto the upholstery foam and use the 40-gauge needle to needle felt the roving until it is very dense. You should end up with a square that's 1½ inches (3.8 cm) for the large charm or 1 inch (2.5 cm) for the small charm.

3 Fold the corners of the square inward and felt them into place, so that the square becomes a rough circle, then felt along the edges so that the circle is more clearly defined.

4 For either the large or small charm, cut a ½-inch (1.3 cm) piece of the light orange roving and split it in half. Roll one half in your hands until it forms a loose ball.

5 Use the 40-gauge needle to attach the ball to the center of the circle, then needle felt along the edges and the top surface of the ball to secure it in place.

6 Divide the circle into five roughly equal wedges, then use the 38-gauge needle to needle felt lines separating the wedges.

7 Continue needle felting until distinct valleys develop, then needle felt along the edges of the valleys. This process gives shape to the separate petals.

8 Flip the piece over and needle felt it from the back. The needle felting should create a small valley on the back and a small hill on the front.

9 Continue working around the flower until the piece looks even.

10 Use the awl to pierce a hole along the back of the charm, then slide in a bobby pin.

GERBER DAISY NECKLACE

FINISHED MEASUREMENTS

Charm/pendant: 2 inches (5.1 cm)

Necklace: 20 inches (50.8 cm)

WHAT YOU NEED

Scissors

48 inches (122 cm) of 100% wool roving in pink

Upholstery foam, 3 inches (7.6 cm) thick

40-gauge felting needle

20 inches (30.5 cm) of 100% wool roving in light orange

38-gauge star felting needle

White beading thread, size D

Milliner's needle or other long sewing needle with a small eye

Matches

2 double-cup knot covers

Flat-nose pliers

1 small sterling silver toggle clasp

WHAT YOU DO TO MAKE THE NECKLACE

To Make the Charm

1 With the scissors, cut a 6-inch (15.2 cm) piece of the pink roving. Split the piece in half and shape it into a rough square by positioning half the roving vertically and the other half horizontally.

2 Place the roving onto the upholstery foam and use the 40-gauge needle to needle felt the wool until it is very dense. You should end up with a square that's 2½ inches (6.4 cm).

3 Fold the corners of the square inward and felt them into place, so that the square becomes a rough circle. Then felt along the edges so that the circle is more clearly defined.

4 Cut a 1½-inch (3.8 cm) piece of the light orange roving and roll it in your hands until it forms a loose ball. Use the 40-gauge needle to attach the ball to the center of the circle. Then felt along the edges of the ball so that it begins to bulk up in the center.

5 Refer to the Gerber Daisy Bobby Pins instructions on page 65 and follow steps 6 through 9 to complete the charm/pendant.

To Make the Beads

1 Cut 26 pieces of the pink roving and 12 pieces of the light orange roving to 1½ inches (3.8 cm) in length.

2 Pull one piece of the pink roving apart (in half) and overlap the two pieces: one half vertically and the other half horizontally.

3 Pull up the corners of the mass and hold onto them with your fingers. Then use the 40-gauge needle to felt the roving into a small ball.

4 Continue needle felting the ball/bead until it holds its ball shape and you've formed a small circular mass approximately ½ inch (1.3 cm) in diameter.

5 Repeat steps 2 through 4 with each piece of roving, pink and light orange, until you've created all 38 beads.

To Assemble the Necklace

1 Cut a 60-inch (152.4 cm) piece of the beading thread, and then insert the thread into the milliner's needle. Fold the thread in half (for strength and thickness) and tie the end of the thread with an overhand knot. Tighten the knot and snip the tail short. With one of the matches, singe the tail so it melts down next to the knot.

2 Thread on a double-cup knot cover so that the opening falls over the knot. Push it all the way to the end.

3 String the beads onto the needle and thread in the following pattern: 1 pink (P) bead, 1 light orange (LO) bead, 2 Ps, 1 LO, 2 Ps, 1 LO, 2 Ps, 1 LO, 2 Ps, 1 LO, 2 Ps, 1 LO, and 2 Ps.

4 String the charm/pendant, pushing your needle through the side of one petal. Then finish adding the beads in the following pattern: 2 Ps, 1 LO, 2 Ps, 1 LO, 2 Ps, 1 LO, 2 Ps, 1 LO, 2 Ps, 1 LO, 2 Ps, 1 LO, and 1 P. Push the beads all the way to the end.

5 Add the second double-cup knot cover with the cup facing away from the beads. Cut the thread to remove the needle. Tie an overhand knot with the two loose pieces of thread, sliding it into place inside the cup. Tighten the knot, clip the tail short, and singe the end with a match.

6 Use the flat-nose pliers to close the cups, making sure your knots are well hidden.

7 Slip one end of the toggle clasp onto the knot cover and close the ring with the pliers. Repeat with the other end of the clasp.

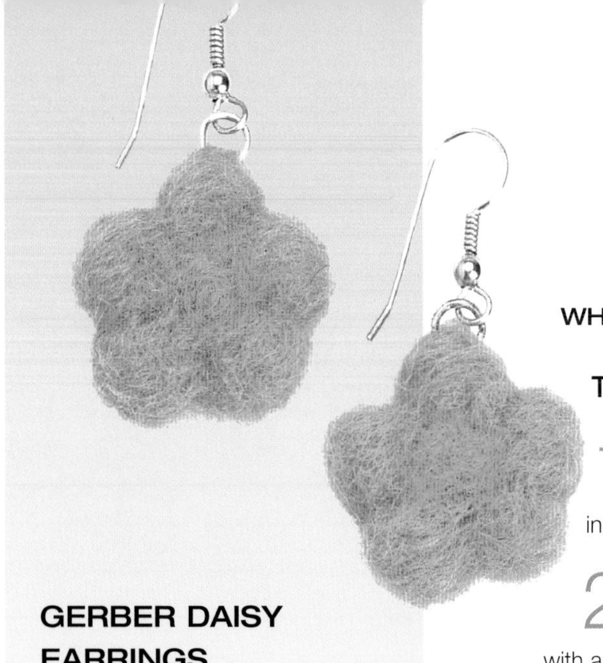

GERBER DAISY EARRINGS

FINISHED MEASUREMENTS

¾ inch (1.9 cm)

WHAT YOU NEED

Scissors

12 inches (30.5 cm) of wool roving in pink

Upholstery foam, 3 inches (7.6 cm) thick

40-gauge felting needle

12 inches (30.5 cm) of wool roving in light orange

38-gauge star felting needle

Awl

Needle-nose pliers

2 sterling silver jump rings, 4 mm in diameter

2 sterling silver French ear wires

WHAT YOU DO TO MAKE THE EARRINGS

To Make the Daisies

1 With the scissors, cut a 3-inch (7.6 cm) piece of the pink roving. Split the piece in half and shape it into a rough square by positioning half the roving vertically and the other half horizontally.

2 Place the wool on the upholstery foam and use the 40-gauge needle to needle felt the roving until it is very dense. You should end up with a square that's 1 inch (2.5 cm).

3 Refer to the Gerber Daisy Bobby Pins instructions on page 65 and follow steps 3 through 9 to complete the flower.

4 Repeat steps 1 through 3 to make a matching flower.

To Finish the Earrings

1 Use the awl to pierce a hole through the top of one of the petals.

2 With the needle-nose pliers, open the jump ring, then slide the ring into the hole in the petal. Close the ring securely.

3 Open the loop on one of the French ear wires. Connect the flower dangle and then close the ring with the pliers.

4 Repeat steps 1 through 3 to finish the matching earring.

This project was completed with:

Wistyria's 100% New Zealand wool roving in Candy (#40) and Tangerine (#48)

Cashmere Thistles Bag

Add subtle sparkle to your wardrobe with this soft, fringed bag. The front flap features a felted motif accented with glistening beads.

LISA CRUSE

designer

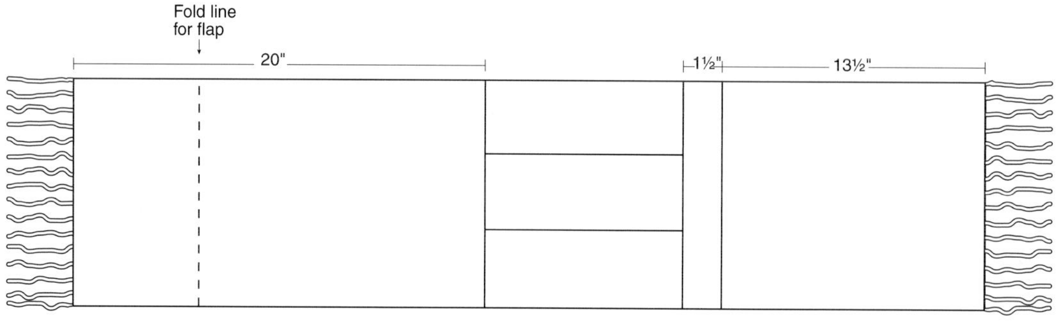

Diagram A

WHAT YOU DO

1 Using the ruler and scissors, measure and cut the scarf according to diagram A, leaving the fringe intact as a decorative element. You now have the pieces for the bag front, the bag back and front flap, and the bottom piece. Save the center sections of the pattern for the strap and sides.

2 Determine the front flap area (the last 6½ inches [16.5 cm] of the longer piece, near the fringe). Place the right side up over the felting sponge, using dressmaker's pins to secure the flap to the work surface along the edges.

3 To make the thistle bulbs, form three ovals by winding the dark green yarn around two fingers for a ball approximately 1½ x 1¼ inches (3.8 x 3.2 cm). Using the 36-gauge needle, needle felt the ovals into position on the front flap according to the design (see detail photo). Try to preserve the rounded form of the bulb as you anchor it securely. With the light green yarn, felt a crisscross design over the bulb, allowing space between the lines as shown.

4 Fill in the design at the top of the bulb with the purple yarn. Using the lavender yarn and leaving short loops as you go, needle felt the flower petals of the thistle for a full, three-dimensional frilled effect (see the project photo).

5 Using the light green yarn, needle felt the stylized leaf pattern around the flower bulbs. (Refer back to the design.) Needle felt the embellishment lines with the brilliant blue yarn. With a sewing needle and carpet thread, securely stitch the beads or sequins in place, stitching the light green beads on the thistle bulbs and blue beads scattered around the felting to balance the design. Refer to the project photo.

SKILL LEVEL
Intermediate

FELTING METHOD USED
Dry Felting

FINISHED MEASUREMENTS
Bag: 11 x 14 x 1 inch (27.9 x 35.6 x 2.5 cm)

Strap: 30 inches (76.2 cm)

WHAT YOU NEED
Ruler or tape measure

Scissors

Wool scarf with fringe, approximately 11 x 54 inches (27.9 x 137.2 cm), excluding the fringe

Felting sponge, approximately 9 x 12 inches (22.9 x 30.5 cm)

Dressmaker's pins

Wool yarn in dark green, light green, purple, lavender, and brilliant blue

36-gauge single felting needle

Thistle pattern (page 123)

Sewing needle

Carpet thread

Glass beads, size 6 to 8, or sequins in light green and brilliant blue

Felt for lining, 36 inches (91.4 cm) wide by 13½ inches (34.3 cm) long

Sewing machine

Steam iron

Magnetic bag closure (optional)

6 Cut the lining pieces from the felt to match the dimensions of the bag front, the bag back and front flap, and the bottom strip (excluding the fringe). Machine baste the bag pieces to the lining pieces ⅛ inch (3 mm) in from the edges. Leave the fringe free, the top edge of the bag front open, and the bottom edge of the bag flap open (especially if you are going to use a magnetic closure).

7 Cut the center scarf portion from step 1 into thirds lengthwise for the strap/sides. Using a ¼-inch (6 mm) seam allowance, stitch together the short ends to form a long rectangle. Form one long tube by stitching a ¼-inch (6 mm) seam lengthwise, right sides together, and then turn the strap to the right side. Press it flat, centering the seam underneath the strap. If necessary, trim its length to 58 inches (147.3 cm).

8 Assemble the bag by first stitching the bottom strip to the front of the bag. Then stitch the bottom strip to the bag's back with the lining sides together, keeping the fringe free and using a ¼-inch (6 mm) seam allowance. Stitch the short ends of the handle/side to the ends of the bottom piece. Using a ¼-inch (6 mm) seam allowance, with the lining sides together, stitch the bag sides to the front from the bottom corners to the top edge. Finally, stitch it to the bag's back/flap, up to the flap fold line. You can finish and reinforce all edges with a machine zigzag stitch.

9 You can place a magnetic closure under the flap, following the manufacturer's directions. Finish the top edge of the front by first stitching the lining to the front and then stitching a zigzag along the edge. For the flap edge, simply flatten the flap against the lining and top-stitch above the fringe, catching the lining edge and leaving the fringe free.

LINDSAY OBERMEYER

designer

Lollipop Bag

SKILL LEVEL
Beginner

FELTING METHODS USED
Dry Felting and Machine Felting

FINISHED MEASUREMENTS
Wet Felted

9¼ x 9¼ inches (23.5 x 23.5 cm) base with a bag depth of 10½ inches (26.7 cm)

14 inches (35.6 cm) from base to handle top

FINISHED MEASUREMENTS
Not Wet Felted

11 x 11 inches (27.9 x 27.9 cm) base with a bag depth of 15 inches (38.1 cm)

19 inches (48.3 cm) from base to handle top

WHAT YOU NEED

Size 6 mm circular knitting needles, 24 inches (61.0 cm) long

7 balls of light-weight, wool-blend, plied yarn in bright green, each 93 yards (85.1 m)

3 stitch markers

Several large stitch holders or one long contrasting yarn as a stitch holder

Materials continued on page 74

Exuberant colors and an easy-to-wear design make this satchel an above-average accessory. It's knitted from basic stitches, and then wet felted in the washing machine. The dots are needle felted on as a final step.

WHAT YOU DO

To Knit the Bag

1 Using the size 6 needles and the bright green wool-blend yarn, cast on 55 sts. Work in the Stockinette Stitch for 11 inches (27.9 cm).

2 Leaving the sts on the needle, pick up another 165 (55 sts for each of the next 3 sides).

3 Join the circle, add a stitch marker to mark the rounds, then continue using the Garter Stitch until you're 15 inches (38.1 cm) from the base. End at the marker.

4 K7, place a marker, K40, place a marker, K2. Place the rest of the stitches on stitch holders.

5 Turn your work. P2, move the marker, P40, P2. Place the final 5 sts on a stitch holder.

6 Begin working in St st. Do decreases on knit rows. Decreases are as follows: K2, move the marker, SSK, knit across remaining sts until the last 2 before the marker, K2Tog, move the marker, K2.

7 End on a purl row when you have only 20 sts remaining.

8 Remove the markers and continue with the Garter Stitch for 27 inches (66.0 cm).

Continued from p. 73

Large-eye needle

Washing machine and dryer

Old plastic bags

Upholstery foam, 3 inches (7.6 cm) thick

Scissors

12 inches (30.5 cm) of 100% wool roving in bright yellow

40-gauge felting needle

12 inches (30.5 cm) of 100% wool roving in light orange

12 inches (30.5 cm) of 100% wool roving in natural

KNITTED BAG GAUGE

5 st and 7 rows = 1 inch (2.5 cm) on size 6 mm needles in Stockinette Stitch (or size to obtain gauge). Take time to check your gauge.

STITCHES USED

Stockinette

Garter

Kitchner

9 Slide the stitches onto the stitch holder. Then slide 111 sts from the left of the decreases onto the knitting needle.

10 Bind off 67 sts, K2, place the marker, K40, place the marker, K2.

11 Turn your work. P2, move the marker, K40, move the marker, P2.

12 Repeat steps 7 and 8. Slide the stitches to a stitch holder.

13 Slide the remaining stitches onto the needle and bind off all of them.

14 Using the Kitchner Stitch, join the band to the remaining 20 sts on the other side of the bag. Sew in all the ends with a large-eye needle.

15 Felt the bag in the washing machine (see Fulling Woven or Knit Wool Yardage on page 20). To ensure that the bag develops a rounded shape, stuff it with crumpled plastic bags and let it air-dry.

To Felt a Circle onto the Bag

1 Slide the upholstery foam into the interior of the finished bag, behind the spot where you want to felt the circle.

2 Cut a 2-inch (5.1 cm) piece of the yellow roving and split the piece in half. Roll one half into a loose ball shape and place the other half over the ball, fanning it out until it loosely covers the ball.

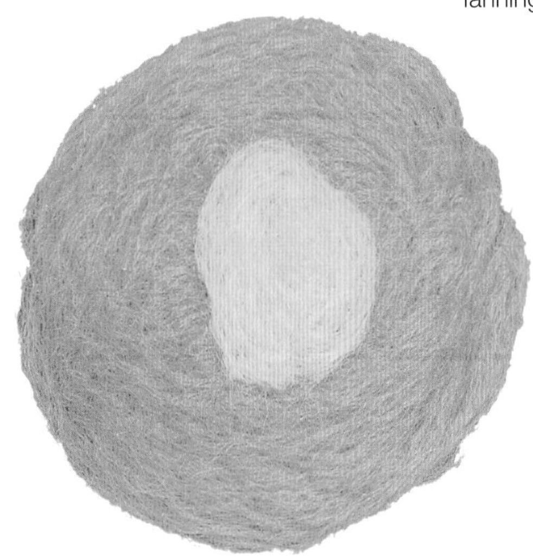

3 Position the ball on the bag, and then use the 40-gauge felting needle to poke around the circle's edge until it's loosely attached to the bag. At this point, check to make sure the circle is where you want it. If necessary, gently pull up the circle, reposition it, and reattach it.

4 You should now have what looks like a large roving bubble. To flatten the bubble, alternate poking between the edges and the interior until you have a uniform circle.

5 Cut a ½-inch (1.3 cm) piece of the light orange roving and split the piece in half. Roll one half into a loose ball shape.

6 Place the light orange ball in the center of the circle you just created, and then place the other half of the roving over the ball, fanning it out until it loosely covers the ball. Use the 40-gauge needle to poke around the edges of the circle until it's firmly attached. Then continue to poke the center dot until it's flat.

7 Continue needle felting across the surface of the circle until everything is flat and tucked into place. The circle should be dense and may feel slightly raised from the surface of the bag.

8 Repeat steps 2 through 7 to make a total of 13 circles, alternating color combinations. Distribute the circles evenly across the surface of the bag, including the bottom.

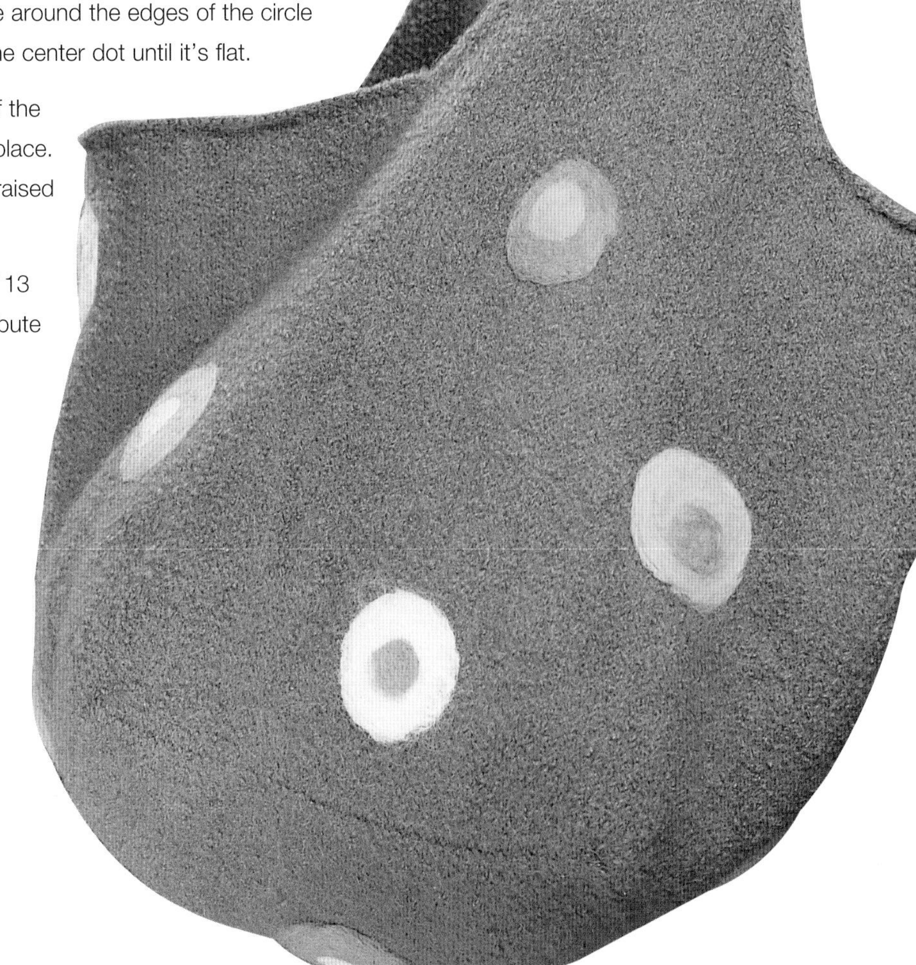

This project was completed with:

Nashua's Julia yarn , 50% wool/25% alpaca/25% mohair, in Ladies Mantle (#3961)

Wistyria's 100% New Zealand wool roving in Tangerine (#48), Natural (#100), and Lemon (#45)

LISA CRUSE

designer

Marbles and Swirls Jewelry Pouch

SKILL LEVEL
Beginner

FELTING METHOD USED
Dry Felting

FINISHED MEASUREMENTS
6 x 9 inches (15.2 x 22.9 cm)

WHAT YOU NEED

2 pieces of wool or wool-blend felt, each 6 x 9 inches (15.2 x 22.9 cm)

Upholstery foam

Swirl design (see page 125)

2 yards (1.8 m) of wool yarn in black

36-gauge felting needle

12 inches (30.5 cm) of satin-faced ribbon, ⅞ inch (2.2 cm) wide

Sewing machine

Carpet thread to match wool felt

Sewing needle

25 to 40 marble design beads

Dressmaker's pins

1 yard (91.4 cm) of satin rattail or twist cord, cut in half crosswise

Just what you need to stash your favorite accessories. Marble beads and needle-felted swirls accent the front of this soft pouch, while ribbon serves as a casing for the satin drawstring—details that make this a bag to treasure.

WHAT YOU DO

1 Place one 6 x 9-inch (15.2 x 22.9 cm) piece of felt on the upholstery foam. Using the swirl design as a guide, needle felt swirls of the black wool yarn into the felt with the 36-gauge needle. Anchor the tail of yarn at the center of each swirl and work your way outward. This felt piece will serve as the front of the bag.

2 Cut the ribbon into two 6-inch pieces to be casings for the bag's drawstring. To form the casings, fold each ribbon end under ¼ inch (6 mm) and machine-stitch the folds in place. Then lay the ribbons ½ inch (1.3 cm) from the top of the bag's front and back, wrong sides together, and stitch along the side edges of the ribbon.

3 Using the carpet thread and sewing needle, hand-stitch one marble bead to the center of each needle-felted swirl on the front of the bag.

4 Place the front and back of the bag together, wrong sides facing in. Pin them together along the edges. Using a ¼-inch (6 mm) seam allowance, stitch just below the ribbon casings, stopping just before the casings on the opposite side.

5 Pull the rattail cords through the casings and knot the ends. Secure them by hand-stitching a bead to each cord end. A few stitches will do the trick.

6 Hand-stitch the remaining beads evenly across the top and bottom edges of the front of the bag.

NIKOLA DAVIDSON

designer

Graphic Eyeglass Cases

SKILL LEVEL
Intermediate

FELTING METHOD USED
Dry Felting

FINISHED MEASUREMENTS
3 ¼ x 6 ½ inches (8.3 x 16.5 cm)

WHAT YOU NEED

- Fiber roving in sheep's wool or alpaca in desired colors, at least 2 ounces
- Upholstery foam, about 10 inches (25.4 cm) square
- Multi-needle felting tool, with 38- or 40-gauge needles
- Single 38- or 40-gauge felting needle
- Embellishments like buttons, ribbon, or embroidery (optional)

Store your glasses in style with these bold, colorful holders. Using the needle-felting tool on the wool until it's dense will make your cases sturdy.

WHAT YOU DO

1 Start by gently pulling your background color fiber apart into tufts approximately 2 ½ inches (6.4 cm) square. Make sure your tufts are wispy and thin. Lay the tufts in a row on the foam backing, making sure they're all facing in the same direction. Continue to lay the tufts in rows, each row slightly overlapping the last. Your tufts of fiber should cover an area that's approximately 7 inches (17.8 cm) square.

2 Now add a layer of tufts on top of the rows you just completed. Place the new layer of rows perpendicular to the first layer. Make sure each tuft is approximately the same size and spaced evenly. Remember to create thin, wispy tufts of fiber for each layer.

3 Create four more layers in the same way, making sure each one is perpendicular to the layer beneath it. You should have six high and fluffy layers of fiber, with no holes or thin spots.

4 With the multi-needle felting tool, punch down through the fibers. The fiber will start to flatten immediately. If it doesn't, try pushing down a bit more firmly with the tool. Punch evenly across the whole area. If you break a needle or chew up the foam, try pushing down more gently.

5 As soon as the felt starts to come together, gently pull the felted fiber away from the foam and flip it over. Continue to needle felt the other side. You should frequently flip the fiber and needle felt both sides; this keeps the fiber from becoming embedded in the foam and helps the foam last longer.

6 Continue using the needle-felting tool until you have a dense, uniform piece of felt. Hold the piece up to the light—if there are thin spots where the light shines through, take a small tuft of fiber, place it over the thin area, and needle felt the fiber in. Be sure to needle felt the area from both sides. Continue to needle felt until you are satisfied with the look and feel of your felt.

7 To make a standard-size eyeglass case, cut the felt into a 6 1/2-inch (16.5 cm) square. If you want to make a narrower case, alter the square as needed.

8 Decorating the eyeglass holder is easy to do while it's still a flat sheet of felt. Use different fibers in complementary colors to create stripes, polka dots, flowers, or other shapes on the piece of felt. To make a polka dot, coil a small piece of fiber between your thumb and index finger. Once you've coiled it to the desired size, place the dot on the felt, then felt it into place with the single felting needle. To make a stripe, gently twist a bit of fiber until it's the desired thickness, and then use the single felting needle to felt it into place. If you don't like the appearance of the dot or the stripe, you can pull it up and reposition it. Once you're satisfied with how the pieces look, use the multi-needle tool to secure them in place.

9 After you've finished embellishing the square of felt, fold it in half. For the classic eyeglass case look, trim the top corner of the non-folded seam, to round it out.

10 Needle felt the bottom and the side of the case, making sure you needle felt both sides of the seam. Test your seam. If it comes apart easily, you need to keep needle felting. The seams should feel sturdy. If you want a seamless look, cut a piece of the foam to fit inside your eyeglass holder and needle felt on top of the seam. Make sure the needles hit the foam underneath but don't come out the other side. Felt the seam from the top and from the sides, alternating between both to make a sturdy seam that won't come apart.

TIP

If you use non-fiber embellishments like buttons, ribbon, or embroidery, be careful not to pierce them with your felting tool. If you add the embellishments before you felt the seams, be sure to keep the embellishments away from the seams.

Nikola Davidson

TIP

Make sure that your tool stays at a 90° angle to the foam backing while you work. This will ensure that you don't break any of the needles.

Nikola Davidson

Tutti Frutti Baubles

Seed beads and colorful fibers brighten up these black spheres. Add a few jewelry findings to the felt balls, and you'll have a terrific new set of accessories in no time.

CANDIE COOPER
designer

SKILL LEVEL
Beginner

FELTING METHOD USED
Dry Felting

FINISHED MEASUREMENTS
Each ball: Approximately ⅞ inch (2.2 cm)

WHAT YOU NEED
6-inch (15.2 cm) square of cardboard

100% merino wool roving in desired colors

10 to 12 felt balls in desired colors, available at most craft stores

38-gauge felting needle

Seed beads, as many as desired in desired colors

Needle and thread to match felt balls

Silk beading thread

Magnetic clasp

Clear nail polish

Ear wires

WHAT YOU DO

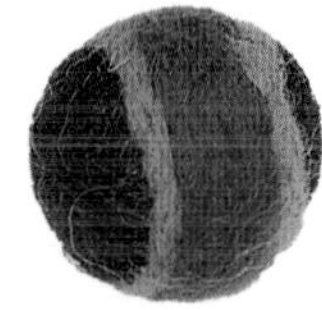

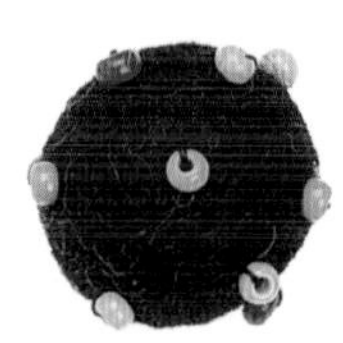

1 Tear off a small sliver of the merino roving and, on top of the cardboard square, begin needle felting one end of it into the first felt ball using the 38-gauge needle. You can start anywhere and design as you go.

2 Continue to needle felt around the ball, twisting the tail of the wool to make stripes, loops, waves, and the like. You can build up as many layers, colors, and thicknesses as you want.

3 To make a polka dot, tear off a tiny sliver of roving and twirl it into a small flat coil. Place the coil on the felt ball and needle felt it into place.

4 To remove needle stab marks from the surface of the design, roll the ball around in your palms for a few seconds. This also helps to reshape the ball somewhat.

5 Stitch seed beads onto the ball with the needle and thread. Anchor your thread first with two forward stitches and one backstitch. String a seed bead onto the needle and sew the needle back down through the anchored spot and out where you want the next seed bead to go. When finished, anchor the thread again and then trim the excess thread.

6 Repeat steps 1 through 5, as desired, to design and needle felt all 10 to 12 felt balls.

7 Thread the needle with a length of silk beading thread slightly longer than the length of the necklace you wish to create. Tie a simple knot approximately 6 inches (15.2 cm) from the end of the thread. Pierce a felt ball with the needle and slip the ball up against the knot. Tie a knot close to the ball on the opposite side. You may need to use a second needle to maneuver the knot close to the ball. Tie a knot where you wish the next ball to sit and pierce a second felt ball with the needle. Slide it into place. Repeat this step until you have the desired number of balls knotted in place on the thread.

8 Securely knot the two magnetic clasp pieces to opposite ends of the necklace. To prevent these knots from coming undone, coat them with a small dab of clear nail polish.

9 To create a matching pair of earrings, thread one or more balls onto silk beading thread, knotting them in place as in step 7. Tie the thread to an ear wire and secure the knot with clear nail polish.

Suiting Bangle

Easy to make, wonderful to wear. This one-of-a-kind bangle is covered in a lining of wool felt that's secured with fabric adhesive. Seed beads and delicate needle-felted details give it old-fashioned elegance.

CANDIE COOPER
designer

SKILL LEVEL
Beginner

FELTING METHOD USED
Dry Felting

FINISHED MEASUREMENTS
The size of the bangle bracelet

WHAT YOU NEED

- Flexible tape measure
- Bangle bracelet
- Scissors
- Fulled wool fabric (see note below)
- Pins
- Upholstery foam pad, large enough to work on
- 38-gauge felting needle
- Hampshire wool roving in desired colors
- Desired pattern for design (see project photo for sample)
- Iron and ironing board
- Embroidery thread (optional, see step 5)
- Seed beads (optional, see step 5)
- Needle and thread
- Sewing machine
- Seam ripper (optional, see step 8)
- Foam paintbrush, 1 inch (2.5 cm) wide
- Multipurpose adhesive
- Glue gun
- Thin strip of wool felt (for bracelet lining)
- Fabric adhesive

WHAT YOU DO

1 Using the tape measure, measure the outside circumference of the bangle bracelet and add 2 inches (5.1 cm). Now measure the width of the bracelet and add 2 inches (5.1 cm). Cut a strip from the wool fabric according to these measurements.

2 To keep your design in the center of the fabric, measure 1 inch (2.5 cm) in from the long sides and mark it with the pins.

3 Place the piece of fabric on top of the foam pad. Starting at one end of the fabric strip and using the 38-gauge felting needle, begin needle felting the Hampshire wool roving in the desired pattern into the fabric, staying within the 1-inch (2.5 cm) borders along the sides. You can add as much or as little roving as you like.

4 Once you're satisfied with the needle-felted design, iron the back of the wool fabric to flatten it out slightly.

5 Optionally, embellish the piece with simple stitching with the embroidery thread and/or with the seed beads, attaching them with the needle and thread.

6 Wrap the strip of fabric around the bangle bracelet, the right side against the bracelet (i.e., the wrong side should be facing outward). Line up the design so it meets end to end-this is where the seam will be. Make sure the fabric is snug around the bangle and pin it in place. Slide the bangle out of the pinned fabric.

7 Use the sewing machine to stitch the two sides together, stitching nearly on top of where it is pinned. Trim away some of the excess fabric, but leave enough in case you need to make an adjustment.

8 Turn the fabric ring right side out and check the fit by placing it on top of the bangle bracelet. It should be taut so it won't slide around. If you need to make adjustments, turn it inside out again and use the sewing machine or the seam ripper to resize it.

9 When you're satisfied with the fit, cut away all the excess fabric next to the seam on the inside. This will keep the fabric from being bumpy or bulky on top of the bangle. If your design doesn't line up, needle felt over the top of the seam to mesh the two sides together.

10 It's nice to have a partner to help you with this step. With the paintbrush, apply a thin layer of multipurpose adhesive over the outside of the bangle bracelet. Stretch the fabric ring over the top of the bangle. Slide the fabric into place so the design is centered, and then leave it to dry thoroughly.

11 Cut a tab-like border along the fabric, and then push the excess fabric into the center of the bangle. This keeps it from being too bulky. Repeat for the opposite side.

12 Push the two tabs into the center and check to make sure they don't overlap and the fabric lays flat. Make adjustments by trimming the tabs so they butt up against each other.

13 Place a dot of hot glue on the inside of the bracelet and stick a tab into place. Hold it down until the glue cools. Repeat for the remaining tabs.

14 To create the bracelet's lining, measure the inside circumference of the bangle bracelet and add 1 inch (2.5 cm). Now measure the inside width and subtract ⅛ to ¼ inch (3 mm to 6 mm)-just enough to make it slightly thinner than the actual bangle. Cut a strip of wool felt according to the measurements.

15 Spread fabric glue over a small section of the wool felt and adhere it to the inside of the bracelet. Smooth out the wrinkles and press into place. Continue working, taking care to spread the glue all the way out to the edges of the wool felt. When you come to the end, trim the felt tail so it meets flush with the opposite end, and then finish gluing. Leave to dry thoroughly before wearing.

MARIE SPAULDING

designer

Passel of Puppy Pins

SKILL LEVEL
Beginner

FELTING METHOD USED
Dry Felting

FINISHED MEASUREMENTS
2 x 1 inch (5.1 x 2.5 cm)

WHAT YOU NEED

White craft felt, 4 x 4 inches (10.2 x 10.2 cm)

Doggie design (see page 123)

Black felt pen

Foam work surface

Wool batting or roving in desired colors

38-gauge star felting needle or 40-gauge felting needle

Sewing needle

Black thread

Two 2 mm black beads

Iron-on adhesive, 4 x 4 inches (10.2 x 10.2 cm)

White canvas or heavy fabric, 4 x 4 inches (10.2 x 10.2 cm)

Iron

Scissors

Scrap fabric, 6 x 6 inches (15.2 x 15.2 cm)

Glue gun

1¼-inch (3.2 cm) pin back

The ultimate accessory for any dog lover. These cute canines are simple to create using your favorite shades of wool batting. In different colors, they can match any outfit.

WHAT YOU DO

1 Place the doggie design (see page 123) on top of the white craft felt and trace it, using the black felt pen for bold lines.

2 Place the craft felt with the design side up onto your foam work surface. Pull off a few small tufts of the wool batting and lay them over the face of the dog so that the wool slightly extends beyond the lines of the design. If you are using roving instead of batting, crisscross the fibers by stacking your tufts in opposite directions as if you were making a sheet of felt (see Needle Felting a Flat Sheet of Wool on page 15).

3 With the felting needle, begin poking along the outline at the top of the head. With the tip of your needle, gently fold the wool fibers that extend outside of the design back toward the center to fill in the face of your dog. Needle felt at various angles to entangle the fibers.

4 Continue this process of filling in the head, including the nose area, by layering tiny tufts of wool, tracing the outline of your drawing by poking your needle along it, and then folding and poking the fibers back into the design area.

5 Using the same method, needle felt the ears with a darker color wool. Needle felt a thin strand of the darker color across the top of the head to connect the ears.

6 To make a nice, round nose, pull off a tiny wisp of the desired color and place it on the bottom of the face. Begin by making a few needle pokes where the center of the nose will be, then use the tip of your needle to twirl the loose fibers and poke them into the shape of the nose. It's easy to make a circle with this method: twirl, poke, twirl, poke, and guide the loose fibers into a circle.

7 By now, the face part of the dog is pretty well attached to your foam work surface. For the best results, do not pull your dog loose from the foam until the design is completely needle felted. You will add the eyes later.

8 Fill in the body with the base color using the same method as you used for the head. Begin with overlapping tufts, and then trace the outline by poking with your needle. Guide fibers toward the center of the design. You'll know you're done when the design is not too flat and not too fluffy. It should have some dimension, but the fibers should not be loose and wispy unless that's the look you desire.

9 Add any spots or surface design to the dog's body. Outline the design with the dark-colored wool by needle felting it into place.

10 Once you are happy with the design, it is time to gently peel the dog from the foam work surface.

11 Now to add the eyes. Thread the sewing needle with a single strand of the black thread. Poke the needle from the back to the front, leaving a 2-inch (5.1 cm) strand at the back of the head. Add the eye bead and run the needle to the back of the design. Tie a knot with the thread ends. Repeat with the second eye bead. Cut the thread.

12 To create a stiff backing for the doggie pin, use the iron-on adhesive to fuse the needle-felted dog to the canvas fabric with the iron. First attach the adhesive to one side of the canvas fabric square, following the manufacturer's directions.

13 Place the scrap fabric on the ironing board to protect its surface. Position the felted doggie face down on the scrap fabric. Next, lay the adhesive side of the canvas square so that it touches the back of your needle-felted design. Follow the manufacturer's directions for the iron-on adhesive to fuse the design to the canvas.

14 Once it has cooled, cut the canvas as close as possible to your needle-felted design.

15 Finally, glue the pin back to your design using a glue gun. Now you're ready for the craft fairs!

Just for Fun

Once you've mastered the simple techniques used in the other sections of this book, you're ready for the more challenging projects that make up this fun-filled chapter. Learn to make pets for the kids to enjoy, needle-felted Easter eggs you can display year after year, and even fanciful, mythical creatures (flying pigs, anyone?) that will melt the hardest of hearts.

LISA CRUSE
designer

Cheerful Cherries Ornaments

SKILL LEVEL
Beginner

FELTING METHOD USED
Dry Felting

FINISHED MEASUREMENTS
Approximately 3 inches (7.6 cm)

WHAT YOU NEED

Protected work surface (cardboard or newspaper layers)

Red wool roving (for the heart)

Polystyrene foam heart form, about 3 inches (7.6 cm) long

36-gauge single felting needle

Multi-needle felting tool, with 36-gauge needles (optional)

Ruler

Scraps of wool roving or yarn in gold, pink, orange, yellow-green, and a snippet of white

Scissors

Green wool roving (for leaves)

Wire cutters

Wire paper clip or florist wire

Craft glue

The perfect way to brighten someone's day. These warm, fuzzy decorations can be assembled quickly using heart-shaped foam forms, bright red wool, and floral wire. Use them to spread a little happiness!

WHAT YOU DO

1 On your work surface, separate the red roving into wisps and fully cover the heart form by alternating the fiber direction in a crosshatch pattern. Needle felt the roving to the form using the 36-gauge single needle or the multi-needle tool.

2 For the cherries, wind lengths of red roving around a fingertip to form a ball about 1 inch (2.5 cm) in diameter, using the ruler to measure. Then needle felt it onto the heart, following the pattern and photo for placement. Keep the cherry form round. Repeat for the second cherry. Shade each cherry by adding wisps of the orange and pink roving or yarn. Add a highlight by felting a single dot of white to the top of each cherry.

3 For the leaves, cut a wisp of the green roving in half crosswise. Mix in the yellow-green roving or yarn for contrast and wrap it around a finger to form a loop, pinching the ends together. Place one loop opposite the cherries on the heart with the pinched ends as the base of the leaf and needle felt it into place, allowing the colors to blend naturally. Form another leaf and needle felt it into place accordingly.

4 Use the gold roving to needle felt the leaf vein and stem. Start toward the tip of the leaf, and then continue down the center, curving in the middle of the heart, and ending at one cherry. Repeat for the second stem. The stems should meet in the middle and connect each leaf cluster to each cherry.

5 To form the hanging loop, use wire cutters to cut the paper clip across the middle or cut and bend a 1-inch (2.5 cm) piece of florist wire to form a U shape. Coat the ends of the wire with craft glue and insert it into the top of the ornament, following the photo for placement. Allow the glue to dry before hanging the ornament.

Polka Dot Pets

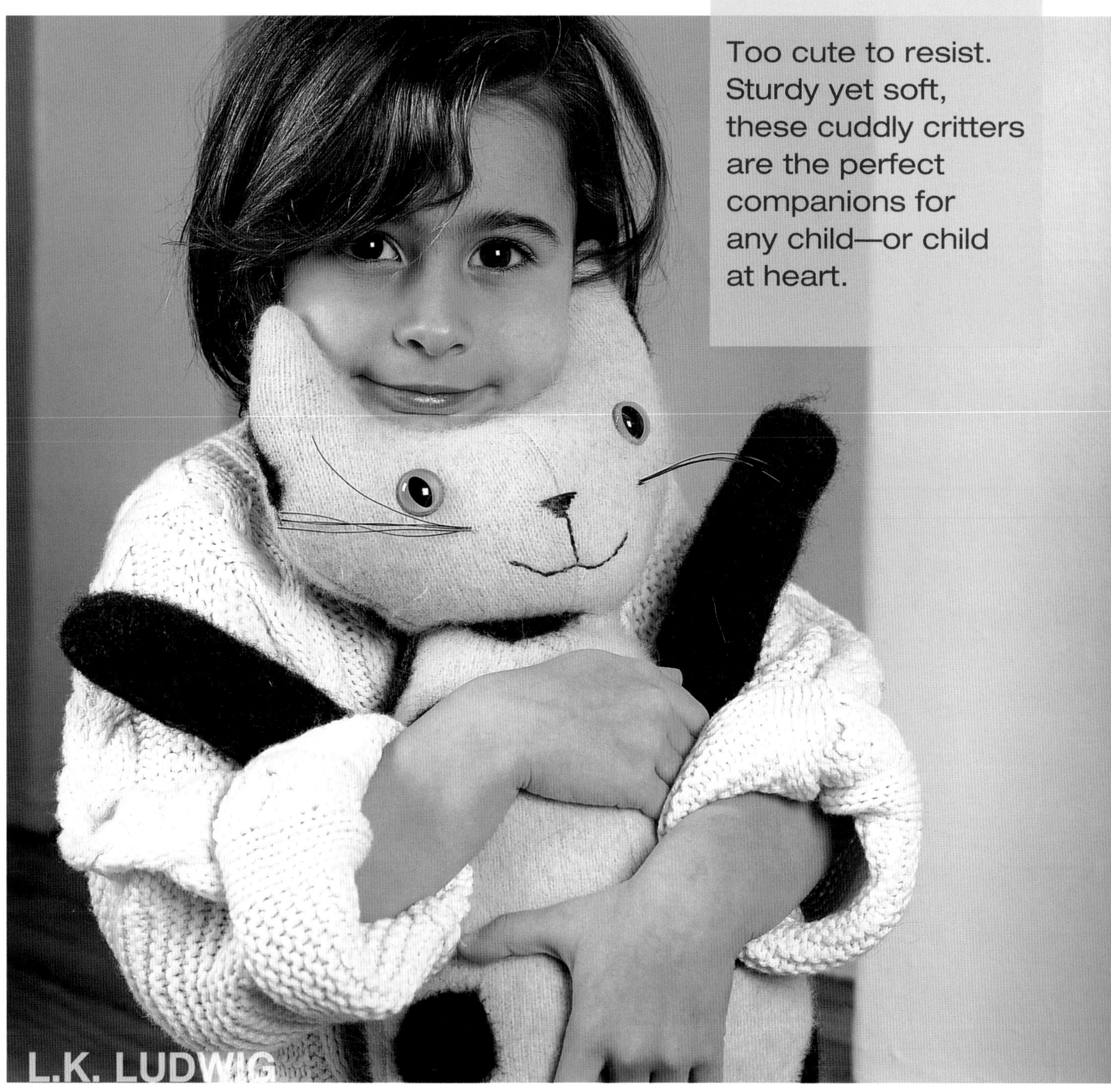

Too cute to resist. Sturdy yet soft, these cuddly critters are the perfect companions for any child—or child at heart.

L.K. LUDWIG

designer

SKILL LEVEL
Beginner/Intermediate

FELTING METHODS USED
Dry Felting and Machine Felting

FINISHED MEASUREMENTS
20 inches (50.8 cm)

WHAT YOU NEED

- 2 wool sweaters (one for each pet), in suitable solid colors
- Washing machine and dryer
- Dog and cat patterns (see page 124)
- Paper and pencil
- Scissors
- Wool roving in accent color(s)
- Upholstery foam or needle-felting mat
- 38-gauge multi-needle felting tool and mat
- Thread to match the sweater
- Sewing needle
- 4 safety eyes (2 for the dog and 2 for the cat)
- Polyester fiberfill
- Straight pins
- Seam ripper
- Embroidery thread in a dark color and needle
- Plastic cat whiskers
- Small piece of felt in accent color (for dog nose)
- Unsharpened pencil

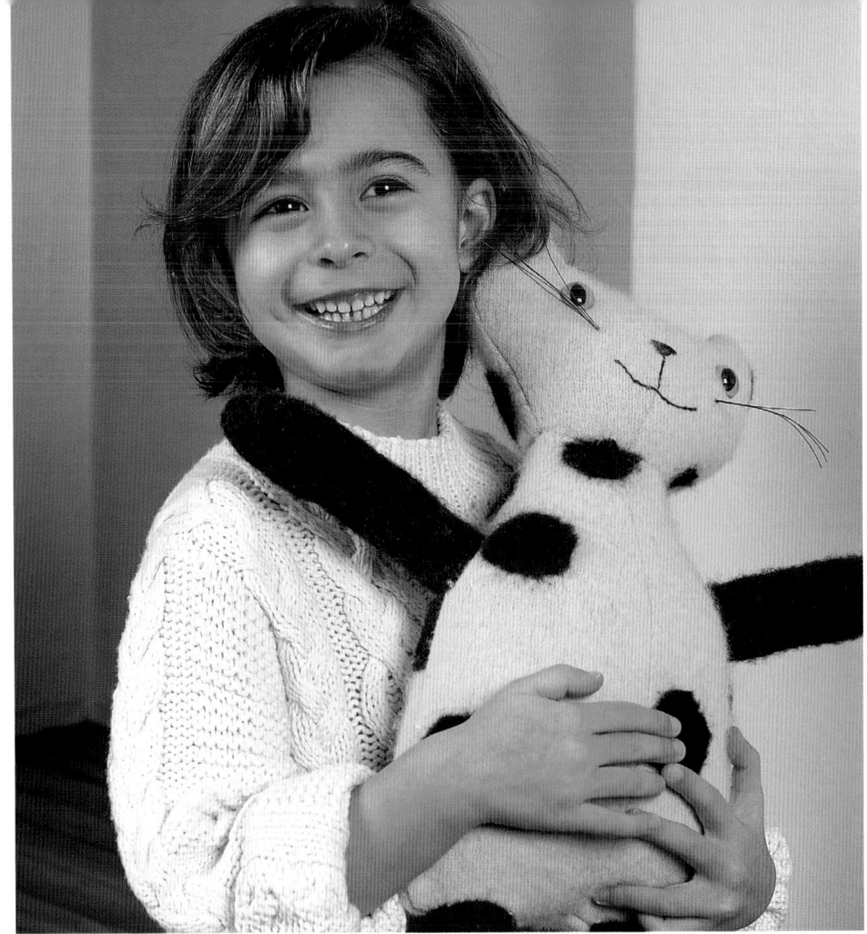

WHAT YOU DO

To Make the Pattern Pieces

1 Full the wool sweaters in the washing machine (see Fulling Woven or Knit Wool Yardage on page 20). Then use the pattern pieces on page 124 to trace and cut out the heads and torsos of the dog and the cat from the sweaters. Remember when cutting two or more pieces off the same pattern piece to reverse the pattern for the second piece. If you're cutting both pieces at the same time, reverse the fabric.

2 To make the spots, tear off four equal-size tufts of the wool roving. Lay one tuft on the upholstery foam, then lay another tuft on top of it, positioned perpendicularly (see Needle Felting a Flat Sheet of Wool on page 15). Then use the multi-needle tool to needle felt the layers together, tucking the edges in as you go so that they make a dot shape. Make as many spots as you like, then set them aside.

3 Use the pattern pieces to assemble one side of each head and one side of each torso, placing the pieces on the foam, right side facing upward, one at a time. Then arrange the polka dots and use the felting tool to needle felt the polka dots to the torso pieces. Don't worry if a good bit of wool fiber pokes through the reverse side.

To Assemble the Polka-Dot Cat

1 Use the matching thread and the sewing needle to sew the pieces of the cat's head together, leaving the bottom of the head open. Insert two of the safety eyes, stuff the head with the polyester fiberfill, and then set it aside.

2 Use the pattern pieces on page 124 to trace and cut out the arms, legs, and tail for the cat from the sweater pieces. Sew the arms and legs together, leaving the tops open for stuffing. Stuff the arms and legs, sew the openings closed, and then set the pieces aside.

3 Sew the pieces of the torso together, leaving openings as marked on the pattern for the arms and legs.

4 Insert the legs into the torso, secure them with the pins, and hand stitch them into place. Do the same with the arms.

5 Stuff the torso, then sew the neck of the torso closed. Insert the neck of the torso into the opening at the bottom of the cat's head, secure it with pins, then hand stitch it into place.

6 Decide where the tail would look best on the cat, then use the seam ripper to open the center seam in the spot where you want to add the tail. Insert the tail and stitch the seam closed.

7 Use the embroidery needle and thread to make a satin stitch for the nose and a chain stitch for the mouth (see detail photo).

8 Trim the plastic cat whiskers until you're left with just a handful. Then use one point of your scissors to poke a tiny hole in one side of the cat's face where whiskers should be. Insert four or five whiskers into the hole and stitch the hole closed. Do the same on the other side of the cat's face.

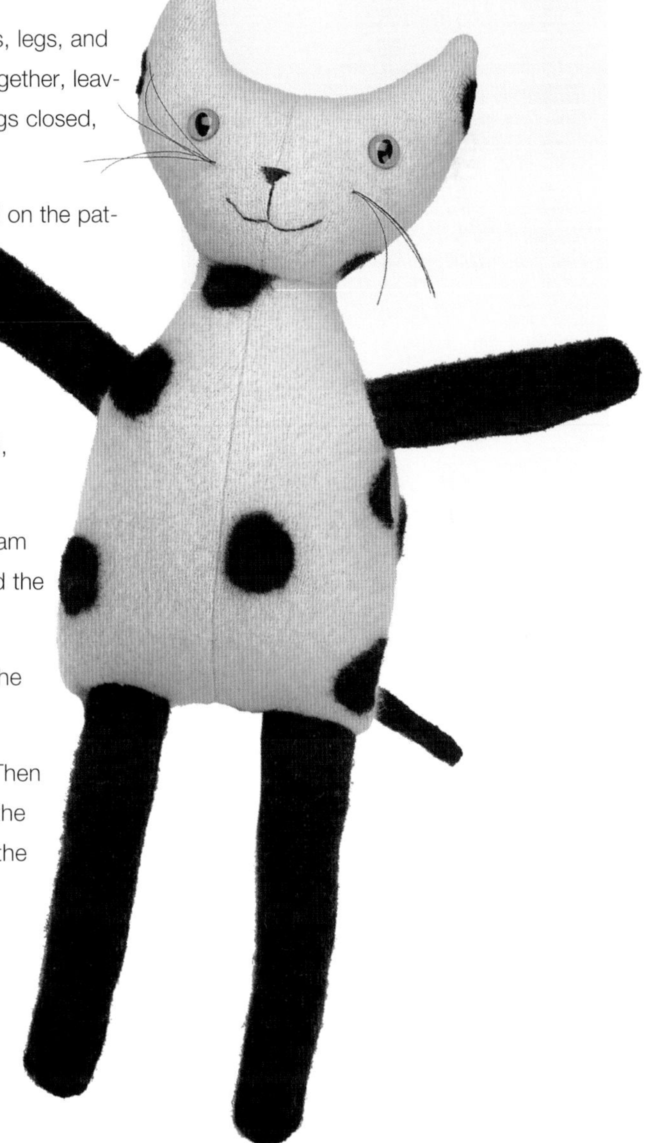

To Assemble the Polka-Dot Dog

1 Use the needle and thread to sew the sides of the dog's head together, leaving openings where the ears will be (see diagram A). Insert two of the safety eyes and then set the piece aside.

2 Use the pattern pieces on page 124 to create the floppy ears from the sweater pieces. Topstitch the ear pieces, wrong sides together. Then slide the end of one of the ears into the slit in the dog's head and stitch it in place. Stuff the head with the polyester fiberfill, then insert the second ear, hand-sew it into place, and sew the head shut.

3 Position the piece of contrasting felt in the place where the nose should be, then use the multi-needle felting tool to needle felt around it, shaping it into a nose and attaching it securely.

4 Use the pattern pieces on page 124 to create out the arms, legs, and tail for the dog from the sweater pieces. Sew the pieces of the arms and legs together, leaving the tops open for stuffing. Stuff the arms and legs, sew the openings closed, and then set the pieces aside.

5 Sew the pieces of the torso together, leaving openings as marked on the pattern for the arms, legs, and neck. Then insert the legs, secure them with the pins, and hand stitch them in place. Do the same with the arms.

6 Stuff the torso, then insert an unsharpened pencil into the neck, making sure the pencil protrudes 2 to 3 inches (5.1 to 7.6 cm) from the neck. Sew the neck closed.

7 Cut an opening into the back of the head (see diagram A again). Then insert the neck of the torso (the pencil) into the head. Pin the neck into place, and sew the opening closed.

8 Decide where the tail would look best on the dog, then use the seam ripper to open the center seam in the spot where you want to add the tail. Insert the tail and stitch the seam closed.

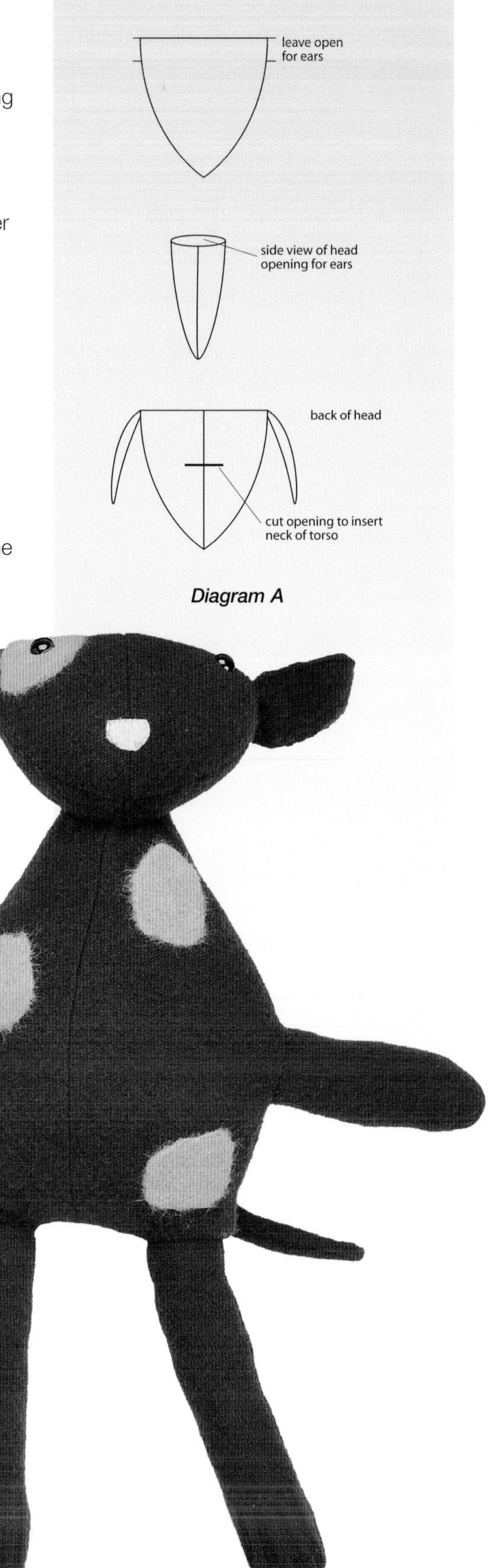

Diagram A

Nesting Photo Album Cover

Customize any photo album with this charming cover. You can needle felt it in a flash using wool roving in natural shades. Then add dry grass or weeds for a finishing touch.

LK LUDWIG

designer

SKILL LEVEL
Beginner

FELTING METHODS USED
Dry Felting and Machine Felting

FINISHED MEASUREMENTS
Book is 12 x 12 inches (30.5 cm x 30.5 cm)

What You Need

One large 100% wool sweater

Washing machine and dryer

Sharp scissors

Book or photo album

Ruler or tape measure

38-gauge needle-felting tool and mat

Designs for the bird, leaves, and nest (see page 123)

Wool roving in colors for the bird, leaves, and nest

A small amount of dry grass or weeds

Paper and pencil

Straight pins

Machine-felted sweater pieces for embellishment

Wire cutters

Safety eye, 6 mm

Fabric that coordinates with sweater, 18 inches (45.7 cm) long

Sewing machine

Needle and thread to match the sweater

WHAT YOU DO

1 Machine felt the sweater according to the instructions (see Fulling Woven or Knit Wool Yardage on page 20).

2 With the sharp scissors, cut the sweater according to diagram A. Remove the waistband if present.

3 Determine the size of the cover by laying the book open on a table and using the ruler to measure its dimensions. Add 10 inches (25.4 cm) to the length and 1 inch (2.5 cm) to the width. This extra material will allow you to create the pockets and provide slack for opening and closing the book.

4 Use the needle-felting tool and mat to needle felt some small sheets of felt in the desired colors for the leaves, bird, and nest. To make the sheets of felt, place four thin layers of the wool roving in a crisscross pattern, layer upon layer, and needle felt the layers into place. Work in the edges. For the nest sheet, sprinkle dry grass into the top layer and felt it in for texture. For the bird, make the beak and wing separately (both are different colors), and then needle felt them onto the bird's body. Finally, cut out the shapes from the felt sheets (based on the designs on page 123) and set them aside.

5 Draw tree branches on the paper. (You don't need to be a skilled artist; tree branches are very irregular, so whatever you draw will be perfect.) Cut out your design and pin it to one of the machine-felted sweater pieces for embellishment. Cut it out.

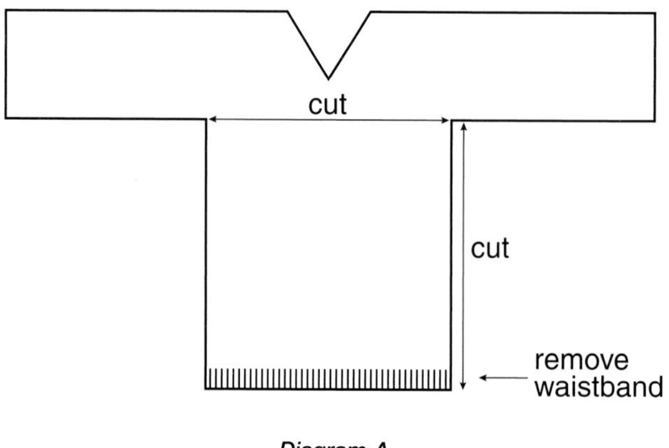

Diagram A

6 Pin the branches into place on the right-hand side of the wet-felted wool sweater piece you cut for the cover in step 2. This will become the front cover. Needle felt the branches into the wool using the needle-felting tool.

7 Next, pin the leaves, nest, and bird into place, and needle felt them into the fabric.

8 With wire cutters, trim the post on the safety eye so it isn't too long. Cut a tiny slit into the bird's head and insert the eye.

9 Fold the color-coordinated fabric so that the wrong side faces out. Cut the fabric to the same size as your cover. Machine-sew this double layer, leaving an opening to turn it right side out. Once you've turned it right side out, hand stitch the opening closed with the needle and matching thread.

10 Pin the fabric to the back side of the cover and topstitch it into place. Give it a ¼-inch (6 mm) seam allowance.

11 Using the book as a guide, fold the sides over the cover boards of your book to form pockets to hold the cover on the book. Pin it into place and topstitch along the same line you used in step 10.

designer

LINDA DIAK

The Gift of Grapes

DECORATIVE GRAPES

SKILL LEVEL
Beginner

FELTING METHOD USED
Dry Felting

FINISHED MEASUREMENTS
3 x 5 inches (7.6 x 12.7 cm)

WHAT YOU NEED

1 ounce of purple wool

38-gauge star or triangular felting needle

Upholstery foam, 1 x 4 x 5 inches (2.5 x 10.2 x 12.7 cm) thick

Small amounts of wool in dark purple, black, lavender, olive green, and brown

Scissors

1 chenille stem, any color

These fanciful bunches look good enough to eat! Wool in shades of purple and black give the grapes dimension. Use the ornament to decorate that special bottle of *vino* you're taking to dinner. The pin is perfect for the lapel of any wine lover.

WHAT YOU DO TO MAKE THE DECORATIVE GRAPES

To Make the Grape Cluster

1 Tear off a tuft of the purple wool that's approximately 3 x 5 x 1 inches (7.6 x 12.7 x 2.5 cm). Shape the tuft into a rectangle, and needle felt it lightly, using the upholstery foam as a work surface. Fold the lower corners of the rectangle into the center so that you form a triangle about 2 x 4 inches (5.1 x 10.2 cm). Needle felt the piece firmly on both sides. This piece acts as the base to which you will needle felt the grapes.

2 To make one grape, tear off a small tuft of the purple wool and roll it into a cylinder that's about 1½ inches wide by ¾ inch thick (3.8 x 1.9 cm). Fold the cylinder in half, pinch the two ends of the cylinder together, and then needle felt the center of the cylinder into a ball shape. Leave the portion in your fingers unfelted and wispy—it will serve as a tail to mount the grape onto the triangle.

3 Repeat step 2 to make 19 more grapes.

4 Beginning at the upper left corner of the inverted triangle, place the first grape so that it hangs slightly over the edge. Needle felt the wispy tail of the grape to

the triangle to secure it in place. Work across the triangle from the left to the right edge. You can mount a grape slightly higher or lower than its neighbor to give the piece more dimension. Fill the triangle with the grapes.

5 To create a shaded effect on the grapes, needle felt a tiny amount of the dark purple wool to the right side of some of the grapes—particularly those in the center and to the right. Then needle felt a few strands of the black wool into the crevices between the grapes.

6 To add a highlight effect on the grapes, needle felt a few strands of lavender wool to six of the grapes to create "a spot of light" (see detail photo). When adding a small dot of color this way, needle felt in the exact area you want the color to appear, then snip the remaining fiber with the pair of scissors.

To Make the Leaf

7 To get a good grape leaf shape, make the leaf in three parts that you'll join together later. First, form a tuft of the olive green wool into a square that's approximately 1 x 3 inches (2.5 x 7.6 cm). Fold it in half and needle felt it lightly on both sides.

8 Fold the two top corners in toward the center and needle felt them down. Then needle felt along the edge to shape the piece into a leaf shape. This will draw the wool in. Needle felt the entire leaf firmly, front and back, to make the piece flat. Then add a small amount of brown wool to the center of the leaf as the vein. Needle felt it into place.

9 Make two more leaf sections in the same way. Then join all three together, overlapping at the base and fanning out a bit (see project photo).

To Make the Vine

10 Wrap the chenille stem firmly in the brown wool. Using small tufts of brown, begin at one end of the stem and wrap, overlapping the wraps as you move down the stem. Each time you run out of fiber, begin the next section by overlapping a bit more. To secure the end of the wrap, wet your fingers, pull out just a few strands of wool from the tuft, and rub in the direction of the wrap.

11 Twist one end of the vine into a coil approximately 1 inch (2.5 cm) long. Hold the vine to the side of the grape cluster and bring the coil to the front. Lay the remainder of the vine across the back of the cluster (see project photo).

12 Place the leaf on the back of the cluster so that it covers the vine, making sure the leaf is still visible from the front of the cluster. Needle felt firmly into the back of the leaf on either side of the vine, being careful not to needle felt directly into the vine, which can cause the needle to break.

13 Use the scissors to trim any stray fibers from the grape cluster and leaves. Be careful, particularly on the leaves, not to cut too closely.

14 You can use the remaining vine to attach the grapes to a wine bottle (or other item, such as a basket handle) by wrapping the vine around the bottle (or handle).

GRAPE PIN

FINISHED MEASUREMENTS

3 x 5 inches (7.6 x 12.7 cm)

WHAT YOU NEED

1 ounce of purple wool

38-gauge star or triangular felting needle

Upholstery foam, 1 x 4 x 5 inches (2.5 x 10.2 x 12.7 cm) thick

Small amounts of wool in dark purple, black, lavender, olive green, and brown

Scissors

1 chenille stem, any color

Pin back, 1 inch (2.5 cm)

WHAT YOU DO TO MAKE THE GRAPE PIN

1 Make the grape cluster as described in steps 1 to 6 (see page 103).

2 Make the leaf as described in steps 7 to 9 (see page 104).

3 Make the vine by following steps 10 to 12 (see page 104).

4 To finish the project, turn the cluster face down, and then lay the pin back across the back, over the base triangle that forms the foundation of the piece.

5 Open the pin, place a small tuft of wool over the pin back, and secure the tuft in place by needle felting it on either side of the pin back. Be careful not to needle into the pin back itself—you could break your needle.

6 Use the scissors to trim any stray fibers from the grape cluster and leaves. Be careful, particularly on the leaves, not to cut too closely.

This project was completed with:

Grafton Fibers, 100% Corriedale wool in Purple, Dark Purple, Black, Lavender, Olive, and Brown

MARIANNE S. DUBOIS

designer

Celestial Mobile

SKILL LEVEL
Advanced Beginner

FELTING METHOD USED
Dry Felting

FINISHED MEASUREMENTS

Moon/star pieces: The crescent moons vary in size, from 2 to 2¾ inches (5.1 to 7.0 cm) in diameter. The attached stars are all about the same size: 1½ inches (3.8 cm) in diameter with points or ½ inch (1.3 cm) in diameter without points. The pieces weigh between 0.6 ounces (for the largest) to 0.2 ounces (for the smallest).

Comet: The head of the comet is approximately 1½ inches (3.8 cm) in diameter. The tail is 5½ inches long by 2½ inches wide (14.0 x 6.4 cm) at the widest point. It weighs 0.3 ounces.

Sun/moon with stars: The core ball is 3 inches (7.6 cm) in diameter. The largest diameter—including the points of the sun across to the attached stars—is 6½ inches (16.5 cm). It weighs 0.5 ounces.

Sun with locks: The core ball for the sun is 2½ inches (6.4 cm) in diameter; with the locks, the total diameter is approximately 6½ inches (16.5 cm). The locks range in length from 2 to 2½ inches (5.1 to 6.4 cm). Its weight is 0.6 ounces.

Sun face: The diameter is about 6¼ inches (15.9 cm), and it weighs 0.5 ounces.

(Marterials Continued on page 108)

Wish upon a star anytime you want with this colorful celestial sculpture. Don't be intimidated by the design—the mobile is easy to assemble using wire and heavy string.

WHAT YOU DO

To Make the Moon/Star Ornaments

1 Cut a length of the floral wire 7 to 8 inches (17.8 to 20.3 cm) long with the wire cutters. Make a small loop at each end with the jeweler's pliers. The loops serve two purposes: they stop the wire from poking through your finished piece and they help anchor the wool so the piece doesn't slide around on the wire.

2 At one end, curve the wire slightly.

3 Wrap the core wool around one loop. Wrap the wool snugly around the wire to create a disc approximately 2¾ inches wide by 1¼ inches (7.0 x 3.2 cm) thick.

4 Working on the upholstery foam, needle felt the wool into place with the 38-gauge needle. Work carefully around the wire. If your needle gets stuck or hits the wire, gently pull it out. Don't twist or pry the needle or it may break. Work it until the piece is firm but not hard. If the piece is now smaller than desired, add another wrap of core wool and needle felt that in. The piece should look something like diagram A.

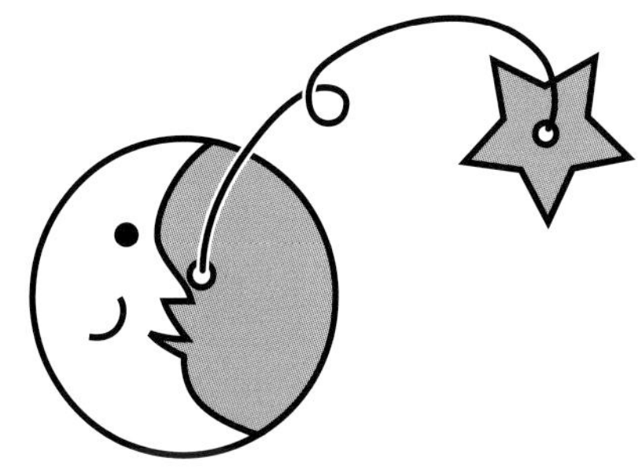

Diagram A

(Continued from page 107)

WHAT YOU NEED

1 package of 20-gauge silver floral wire

Wire cutters

Jeweler's pliers

3 ounces of desired core wool, any type, white or light gray

Upholstery foam

38-gauge star felting needle

Colored wools, about 4½ ounces total, depending on the number of pieces (colors can include pearl gray, dark blue, black, variegated green, yellow, and gold)

Small multi-needle tool with two-to-four 38-gauge needles (optional, for shaping the core wool or applying the colored wool)

Gold or silver seed beads and a beading needle (optional)

40-gauge felting needle

White wool, 1 x 1 inch (2.5 x 2.5 cm)

Heavy string in black or silver (to connect the mobile pieces)

Silver-colored metal ring (or a ring spray-painted silver, black, or white)

Fishing line or other transparent thread (or silver or black thread)

Long sewing needle

Fabric glue

Material Notes: You use a very small amount of wool for each piece. For example, you might use less than 0.5 ounce of core wool and 0.2 ounce or less of colored wool for any one piece.

5 With the wire extruding from the top of the disc, shape some of the pearl gray wool into a crescent on your disc. Make sure you use a thick enough layer to cover the core wool thoroughly, but don't needle felt it completely into place just yet. Fill in the rest of your disc with the dark blue wool. The crescent can face left or right.

6 Along the join between the colors, fashion a gray nose profile sticking into the blue. Below the nose, form the upper lip shape and a curve for the mouth. Widen this curve with a little more of the blue wool.

7 Now needle felt the blue and gray wools firmly into place over the whole of the disc.

8 Just in from the bridge of the nose, add a small bit of blue wool for an eye, and then add a black-wool eyebrow above it. About even with the tip of the nose, and under the eye, add a small puff of gray wool for a cheek. If you want, underline the bottom of the cheek with a thin line of blue wool.

9 At the loop on the other end of the wire, wrap a small amount of core wool to make the center of the star. Needle felt this into place. The diameter should be about ½ inch (1.3 cm). If you don't want points, just cover the star in the colored wool of your choice. If you want points, make five tufts of wool about the size of a 50-cent piece. Fold each into a small triangle, and needle felt them into shape, leaving the bases of the triangles un-needled. Spread the triangles out along the perimeter of the ball, and needle felt them into place. (Careful! These pieces are small, and it is easy to poke your fingers while making and attaching these small bits.)

10 Curve the wire between the moon and the star to form a small loop. Make the loop closer to the moon than the star so the piece hangs properly. Adjust the wire curve between the moon and star so the weight is distributed evenly.

To Make the Comet

1 Cut a length of wire 7½ to 8 inches (19.1 to 20.3 cm) long and make a small loop at each end.

2 Wrap core wool around one loop to make a ball 1½ inches (3.8 cm) in diameter. Cover this ball with colored wool (I used a variegated green) that adds contrast to the yellow you'll use in the comet's tail.

3 To determine the balancing point along the wire, first loosely wrap the amount of wool you estimate you'll need for the tail around the wire. When you've found the balancing point, make a loop in the wire there (see diagram B).

4 With the 38-gauge needle, begin needle felting the wool for the tail. Unless you are making a very large comet, you don't need to use core wool; just use the desired color (I used yellow). Shape the tail so it's narrow near the ball and wider at the end. I created mine somewhat feather-shaped. Make sure the wire's hanging loop sticks out along the top of the tail.

5 Optionally, add gold or silver seed beads to the tail to add some sparkle (stitch these in place with the beading needle and thread).

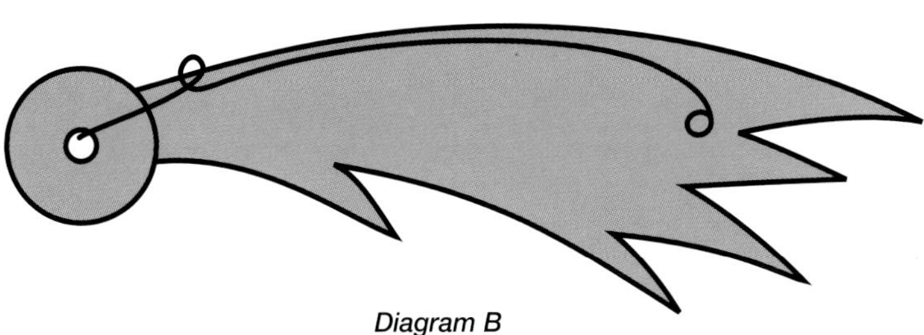

Diagram B

To Make the Sun with Locks

1 Make a ball about 3½ inches (8.9 cm) in diameter for the core of the sun out of the core wool.

2 Cover this with yellow wool and needle felt it into place with the 40-gauge needle.

3 Add a face to one side of the ball (see the directions below for how to make a face).

4 With the face toward you, add locks around the sun, encircling the face. If your locks are long, fold them in half and needle felt them into place in the middle with the 38-gauge (or coarser) needle. If your locks are shorter, needle felt one end in place and keep adding locks. Vary the colors and lengths a bit as you go around.

To Make the Sun/Moon Ornament

1 Cut a piece of floral wire 11½ to 12 inches (29.2 to 30.5 cm) long. Make a small loop in the middle of the wire. Curve the entire length in a gentle arc.

2 Wrap core wool around the loop until you have made a ball that is 3¼ inches (8.3 cm) in diameter when firmly needle felted.

3 Position the ball so you have wire sticking out the top and bottom, each curving to the same side (see diagram C). Make small loops on each end of the wire.

4 With the wires curving to the right, cover the left half of the ball in the yellow wool and the right half in the pearl gray wool.

5 Add a face, putting the nose over the border between the colored wools. Make the eyelid on the sun side with yellow wool and on the moon side with gray wool.

Diagram C

6 Make four or five triangular pieces to be the rays for the sun side (each 1½ inches [3.8 cm] long and about 1 inch [2.5 cm] wide at the base). These are larger versions of the triangles you made for the small suns on the moon/star ornaments.

7 Wrap small balls of core wool on the loops at each end of the wire. Make small stars as you did for the moon/star ornaments.

8 To determine the balancing point, you may have to reshape the curves in the wire. Once you've found the balancing point (likely to be near where the wire exits on the top of the ball), make a loop for hanging the piece.

To Make the Sun Face

1 Make a slightly flattened disk out of core wool, 3½ inches (8.9 cm) wide.

2 Add a base color, such as yellow or gold.

3 Make a face on one side, following the directions below.

Face: Start with the nose, the mouth, and (optionally) the chin. Then, do the eyes and the cheeks. Attach all the parts, and then do the final shaping. Use the 40-gauge needle; a finer needle will leave smaller holes than a coarser needle.

Nose: Fold in half lengthwise a tuft of wool about 2 inches long and 3⁄4 inch wide (5.1 x 1.9 cm). The folded end will be the nostril end of the nose, and the torn end will make the bridge of the nose and the eyebrows. Then fold the long edges in toward the center (diagram D).

Place this piece so the bottom of the nostril end is about halfway down the head (or slightly more). The brow ridge should end about one-third of the way down

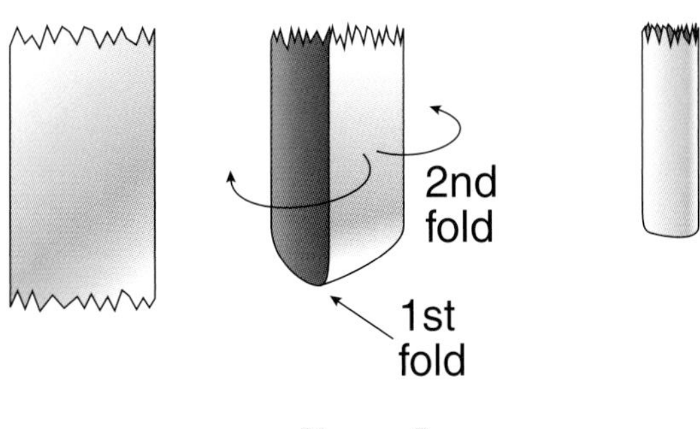

Diagram D

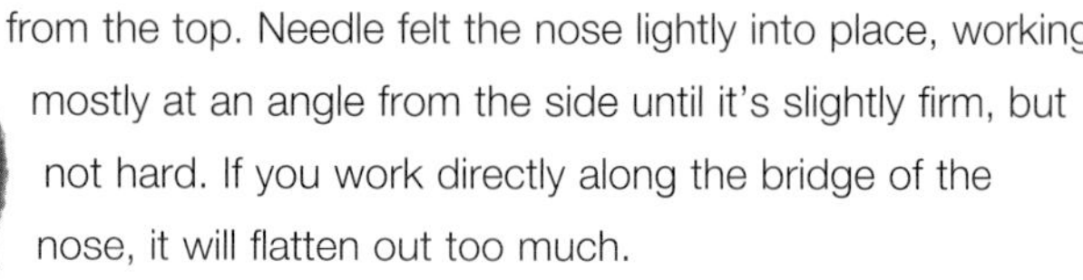

from the top. Needle felt the nose lightly into place, working mostly at an angle from the side until it's slightly firm, but not hard. If you work directly along the bridge of the nose, it will flatten out too much.

Shape the nostrils by needle felting around the lower part of the nose. To make prominent nostrils, needle felt a small, soft ball of the same color wool on both sides of the nose at the base. Cover with a small amount of extra wool if the creases are too prominent.

Eyes: Needle felt both sides of the upper nose to make slight indentations for the eyes. With a small amount of white wool, make two oval shapes and needle felt them into the indentation about one eye's width apart.

Make two small circles of colored wool for the iris (which ranged from 1⁄16 inch to ½ inch [1.6 mm to 1.3 cm] in my pieces). Dark blue wool makes a nice eye color, but you can use any color you want. Needle felt one into the center of each oval. To the blue circle, add an even smaller black dot for the pupil. At about 10 o'clock on the border between the iris and the pupil, add a tiny dot of yellow ("the spark"). Needle felt the spark at the same point for both eyes; otherwise, the face will look wall-eyed.

Next, fold a small tuft of face-colored wool in half to make an eyelid. It doesn't have to be very wide. Needle felt it separately so it holds together. Needle felt slightly more at the fold and less at the fuzzy end. Repeat to make two identical eyelids. (Hint: Before you place them on the face, make all four so they look about the same.) Place the straight end over the eye and needle felt the fuzzy end into place above the eye. Repeat for the lower lid. Then repeat for the other eye.

Eyebrows: You can either use the end of the wool that makes up the bridge of the nose or add wool in an arc over the eyes. Eyebrows can be the same color as the face or a contrasting color.

Lips: There are two ways to make lips. You can twirl a small tuft of wool (as wide as desired) around a thin smooth object such as the smooth end of a felting needle or a shish kabob skewer. The tuft should be slightly thicker in the middle and taper to the ends. When you've twirled the wool enough for it to keep its shape, slide it off the needle shaft. You can then needle felt it into place as a top lip, a bottom lip, or both.

To make a flatter lip, fold a tuft of wool over as you did for the nose and eyelids. If you fold the wool over a shish kabob skewer, needle felt the folded piece right behind the stick, then slide the piece off the stick and needle felt the piece near the edge. This creates a very straight edge. Make a second lip the same way or combine with a rolled lip (see above). Needle felt the fuzzy end of the top lip below the nose, and then add the lower lip.

To add a goatee (a triangular wedge of wool needle felted under the lips, but hanging free over the chin), don't needle felt the fuzzy end of the lower lip. If you used a rolled lip as the bottom lip, add a fuzzy bit of wool to the chin area.

The last step is to add a darker color inside the mouth. Open the lips a bit and stuff in a color (black is usually too dark). Needle felt the wool into place. For suns, I prefer a dark orange or red, or blue if I've used that in the eyes.

Cheeks: Fold two tufts of wool into pillow shapes. Place one on each side of the nose below the eyes. Needle felt them lightly into place with the 40-gauge needle. You can even add a little contrasting color to the cheeks.

Now go back over your piece to make sure everything is needled securely in place. This is the time to give final shape to the eyes, nose, mouth, and cheeks to get the desired expression.

4 Next, make six to eight rays to place around the edge of the face. Make these triangular pieces the same way you made the rays for the moon/star ornaments. Needle felting them to the edge of the face with the 40-gauge needle. When finished, they should be about 1½ inches long by about 1¼ inches (3.8 x 3.2 cm) at the base. If you use a contrasting color (I used violet), needle felt them neatly into place since they won't blend in. You can also add swirls of the contrasting color onto the sun face.

To Make the Mobile

1 Using the heavy string, tie two lines across the wire ring to break the circle into quarters (so it looks like an X). Temporarily add a loop of string to the X so you can move the balance point of the hanger. As you add ornaments around the circle, you'll have to balance them, so don't make a permanent hanger until you have the balance point worked out.

2 Use invisible fishing line to hang the ornaments. Decide how far down the line you want the ornaments to hang. Measure and cut double the length. I used line 17 inches (43.1 cm) long, doubled to 34 inches (86.4 cm). String the line through the loops on the ornaments, making a long loop of line. Tie the ends together. For the ornaments without loops (such as the sun with locks), thread a

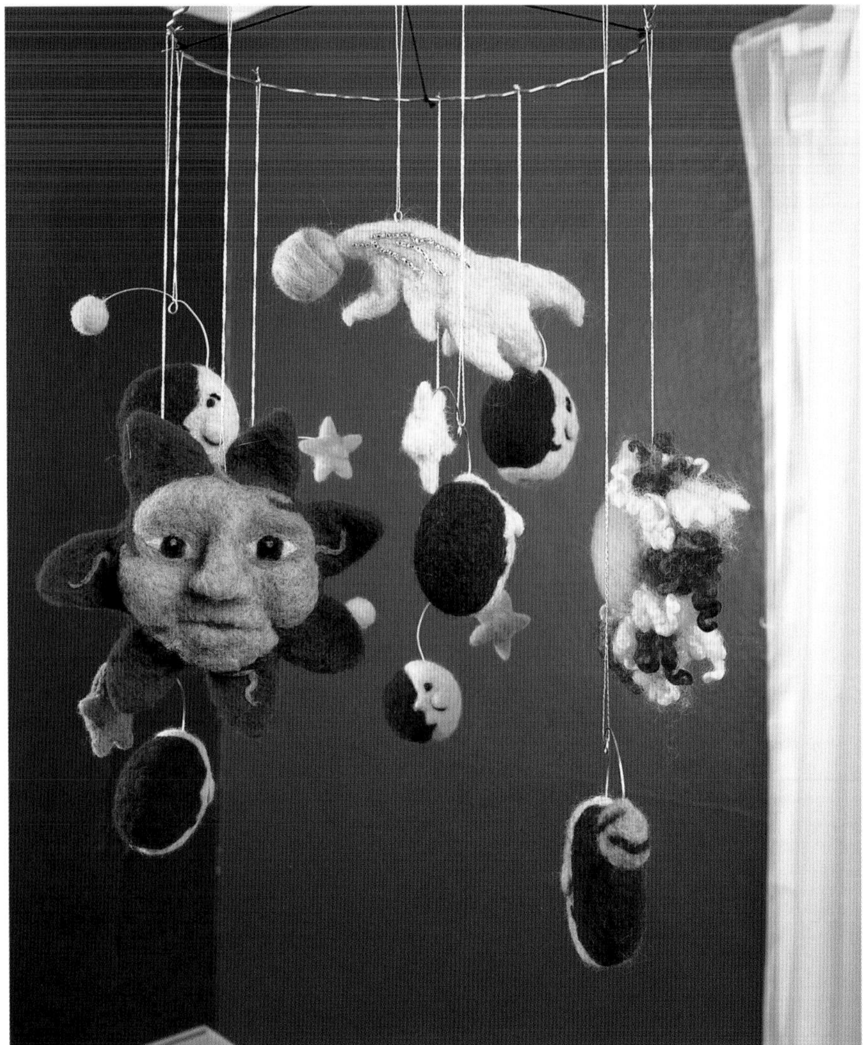

This project was completed with:

Halcyon Yarn Dorset, Suffolk, or Hampshire wool

Ashford Corriedale Fiber in Marigold (bright yellow) and Tangerine (orange)

Harrisville wool in Marigold, Cornsilk (soft yellow), Gold, and Melon (orange)

Chickie Masla Peace Fleece, a yellow and orange mix containing mohair

Harrisville wool in Iris (dark purple), Pearl (pale gray), and Royal Blue (dark blue)

Miriam Carter short staple merino batt in Electric Blue (blue)

Spinner's Hill Farm dyed locks in yellow, orange, and red

long needle (I used a doll maker's needle), sew down from the top of the piece, exit the bottom, and then return back up through the piece to the top again. This will make a loop you can tie like other ornaments.

3 Lay the top of the loop (at the knot) across the wire. Pull the ornament through the loop, creating a half-hitch. Space the ornaments around the wire, sliding the half-hitches to move ornaments. Hold up the wire by the hanging string loop, moving the pieces until the wire is balanced horizontally. Knot the hanging loop, and then add a touch of fabric glue to the half-hitches to keep them in place.

Pigs Do Fly!

Here's a fun project if you're ready to tackle a three-dimensional design. Make the basic forms with core wool, then join and cover them with fine, colored wool. If you ever said you'd take up needle felting when pigs can fly, you're now out of excuses.

SUZANNE URBAN

designer

SKILL LEVEL
Intermediate

FELTING METHODS USED
Dry Felting and Wet Felting

FINISHED MEASUREMENTS
6 inches long by 4 ½ inches tall (15.2 x 11.4 cm)

WHAT YOU NEED

2- to 4-ounce batt of natural core wool

Upholstery foam

2 36-gauge triangular felting needles

Scissors

2- to 4-ounce batt of rose-colored wool

38-gauge star felting needle

Pipe cleaner

Skewer or paintbrush

Wing pattern (see page 123)

Paper and pencil

1 sheet of wool felt in muted blue, muted green, and soft yellow

Fabric glue

2 strands of 32-gauge florist wire, each 4½ inches (11.4 cm) long

1 strand of 32-gauge decorative wire, 7 inches (17.8 cm) long (for the hanger)

1 wooden bead big enough to hold the decorative wire

Sewing needle and coordinating thread (optional)

WHAT YOU DO

To Make the Pig's Body

1 Pull some wool from the core batt, roll it up into a loose roll, and place it on the upholstery foam. With the two 36-gauge needles, needle felt the loose roll into a kidney bean shape that's roughly 3¼ inches long by 1¼ inches wide (8.3 x 3.2 cm). Add more wool if you have to, and needle felt it in. As you punch the needles into the wool, rotate them to create the kidney bean shape. Make the top side of the kidney bean slightly larger than the bottom (see diagrams A and B). The indented curve of the kidney bean will serve as the back of the pig, while the underside will serve as his tummy.

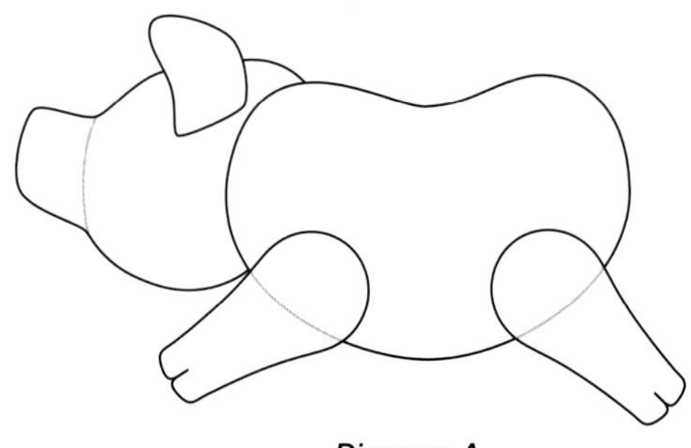

Diagram A

To Make the Legs

2 Pull some more wool from the core batt, loosely roll the wool into a funnel shape, and place it on the foam. Again using the 36-gauge needles, needle felt the funnel into a drumstick shape about 2 inches (5.1 cm) long (see diagram C). You don't have to needle felt firmly, because the shape and size of the leg can be adjusted as you work on the pig.

3 Repeat step 2 to make three more legs. Don't worry if all of the legs aren't exactly alike.

To Make the Head

4 Pull more wool from the core batt and roll it into a ball shape. After placing it on the foam, loosely needle felt the form into a uniform ball. Then needle felt the back side of the ball so that it's flat. You should end up with a shape that resembles the top of a mushroom, measuring 2 to 3 inches (5.1 to 7.6 cm) in length (see diagram D).

To Attach the Head and Legs to the Body

5 Place the flat side of the mushroom shape onto the larger end of the kidney bean, and then needle felt around the edges of the head into the kidney bean. Needle felt the head down until its shape is in scale with the body. Then needle felt two holes in the front of the head to serve as guides for placing the eyes.

6 Place one of the drumstick-shaped legs against the body, so that the head of the drumstick touches the body at a slight angle (so that the pig appears to be flying). Then needle felt loosely around the top of the leg into the body. Repeat with the other three legs. Once you're satisfied with the placement of the legs, needle felt them more firmly to the body. The pig should be able to stand on its own.

To Make the Snout

7 Pinch off 2 inches (5.2 cm) of wool from the core batt and roll it up with your fingers. On the foam, loosely needle felt the roll so that it's about 1 inch (2.5 cm) long. Place one end of the roll between the eyeholes on the face of the pig. Hold the roll in place and needle felt firmly around its base; it will serve as the pig's snout. If the roll is too big, snip off some of the wool with scissors and needle felt the loose ends in. If it's too small, add more wool, needle felting it in to make the piece larger (see diagram E).

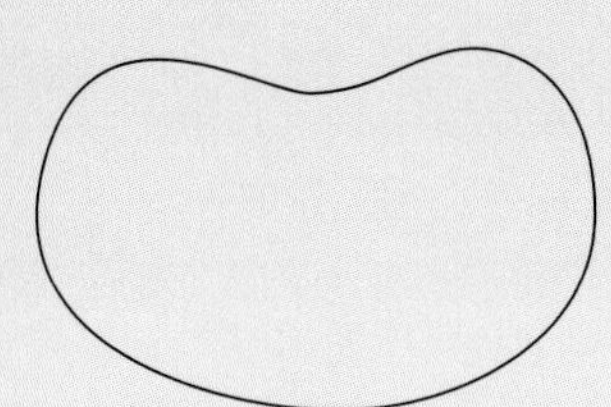

Diagram B

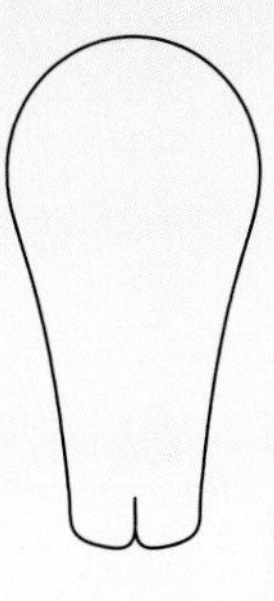

Diagram C

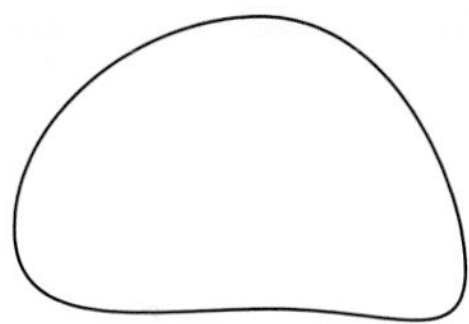

Diagram D

Diagram E

TIP

If you aren't satisfied with where you placed the legs, simply pull them out gently and reattach them to the body.

Suzanne Urban

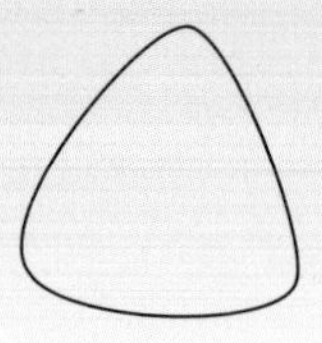

Diagram F

Diagram G

8 Pause a moment to take stock of your pig: If you want him to have more of a tummy, needle felt in more wool. Do the same to any of the body parts that you feel need added bulk. Take a minute to needle felt the attached parts more firmly to the body (see diagram A again).

To Make the Ears

9 Pinch off 2 inches (5.1 cm) of wool from the core batt and place it on the foam. Roll the piece into a rounded triangle shape with your fingers, and then use the 36-gauge needle to needle felt the piece down into a firm shape that will serve as an ear. Leave the base of the piece loose, so that you can easily attach it to the head later. Needle felt the middle area well, to create a depression that indicates the inside of the ear (see diagram F). Repeat this step to make a matching ear.

To Color the Pig

10 Once you've fully assembled the pig, take a few strands of the rose-colored wool and wrap them around the pig's middle. Then use the 38-gauge needle to punch the rose-colored wool down so that it covers the core wool. In this way, "color" the entire body with the rose-colored wool. In tight spots like the ears, gently tap the wool onto the ear so that it adheres, then increase the depth of your needling to cover the core wool.

To Make the Eyes

11 Use the 38-gauge felting needle to punch two slanted lines into the face.

12 Making the eyes should give you a good idea where to place the ears. Needle felt the ears onto the head.

To Make the Feet and the Tail

13 For the feet, hold the pig upside down and punch a line across the bottom of each foot (see diagram C again).

14 To make the tail, wrap rose-colored wool around the pipe cleaner from top to bottom. Then wet your hands with warm water and soap, place the pipe cleaner between your hands, and roll it back and forth. This rotating motion will make the wet wool felt cleanly onto the pipe. If some wool comes off, wrap more around the pipe cleaner and repeat the process until the wool feels hard and is securely fused to the pipe cleaner (see diagram G).

TIP

You can also loop the wire on end and secure it to pig's back between the wings by sewing the loop to the center of the wing where wool secures the wing to the pig's back.

Suzanne Urban

15 After the pipe cleaner dries, curl it around a thin rod such as a skewer or the end of a paintbrush. Cut about a 1½-inch (3.8 cm) length to serve as a curly tail. Hold one end of the curled tail against the bottom of the pig, add some rose-colored wool around the base, and needle felt the wool around the tail, into the bottom of the pig.

To Make the Wings

16 Trace the wing pattern on page 123 onto a sheet of paper and cut it out. Fold the blue piece of wool felt in half. Align the bottom edge of the paper wing with the folded edge of the felt. Trace around the paper wing, transferring the shape to the felt. Then cut the shape from the felt, leaving the folded edge intact. Repeat this step to make the second wing.

17 Apply the fabric glue inside each wing. Place one of the 4½-inch (11.4 cm) lengths of florist wire in the middle of each wing, and then close the wings, sandwiching the wire inside. Let the wings dry.

18 After the wings dry, bend them in the middle so that both side curve upward. Place the base of the wings on either side of the middle of the pig's back. Add some rose-colored wool to cover the bases—in the middle of the pig's back—and needle felt the wool into the back of the pig, so that the wing stays in place. You should be able to pick up the pig by either wing.

To Add the Wire Hanger

18 Wrap the 7-inch (17.8 cm) length of decorative wire around the pencil. Add one of the wooden beads to one end of the wire, and then bend the wire to keep the bead in place. Slip the other end of wire beneath the wool holding the wings in place, and bend the wire into a small loop so that it can't slip out. Add more rose-colored wool on top of the wire loop and needle felt the wool down into the pig's back to further secure the wire. The wire should stand straight up on its own. See detail photo.

BARBARA CRAWFORD

designer

Easter Eggs

These colorful eggs make a striking decorative accent at any time of the year. And don't worry—they won't crack. Each egg is made from an easy-to-felt foam form that you can embellish as much as you like.

EXPERIENCE LEVEL
Beginner

FELTING METHOD USED
Dry Felting

FINISHED MEASUREMENTS
1 5⁄16 x 3 1⁄16 inches (3.3 x 7.8 cm)

WHAT YOU NEED

38-gauge single triangular felting needle

Small multi-needle tool with 38-gauge triangular needles

10 to 12 balls of roving, each ½ ounce, in coordinating colors

6 polystyrene eggs

Designs for decorating the egg (try creating your own)

Paper and pencil

Scissors

Pins

WHAT YOU DO

1 Use the 38-gauge single or multi-needle tool to needle felt roving around the entire egg (see Covering a Polystyrene Foam Shape on page 17). Cover the surface of the egg with a base color of your choice.

2 Use strands of wool in different colors to create stripes (or even zigzags). Overlap stripes with outlined diamond shapes. Fill in some of the diamond shapes with coordinating or contrasting colors using a the single needle tool.

TIP

When using a multi-needle tool on a polystyrene foam form, be careful not to poke too many holes in one area, as the foam will break down. Use the multi-needle tool to smooth the surface.

Barbara Crawford

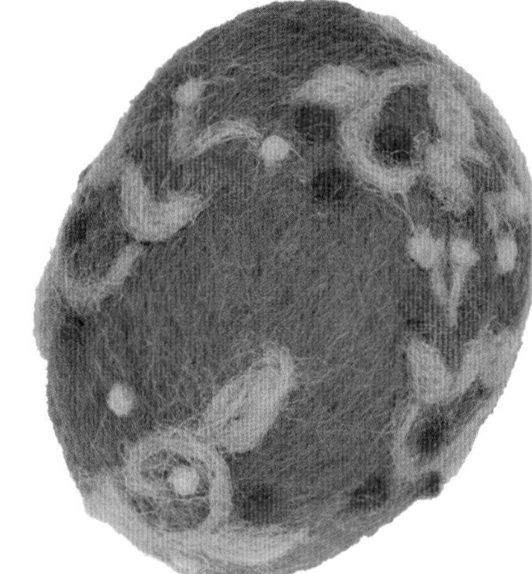

3 Create a circle by pulling off a very small piece of wool and rolling it into a ball with your fingers. Lay it on the egg, and poking it in with a single needle. You can use the needle to refine the circle. The zigzags are lines of wool that I pulled off and shaped in the same fashion

4 If geometric designs aren't what you have in mind, create floral designs. Create flower patterns on paper, cut out them out with scissors, and secure them to the egg with a straight pin. Outline the design with wool, remove the pattern, and fill in the petals. You can also create flowers freehand by pulling out a small tuft of the wool to use for the petals. Roll it between your fingers to get the desired shape and then needle felt it on the surface of the egg. Create buds, stems, and vines in the same way.

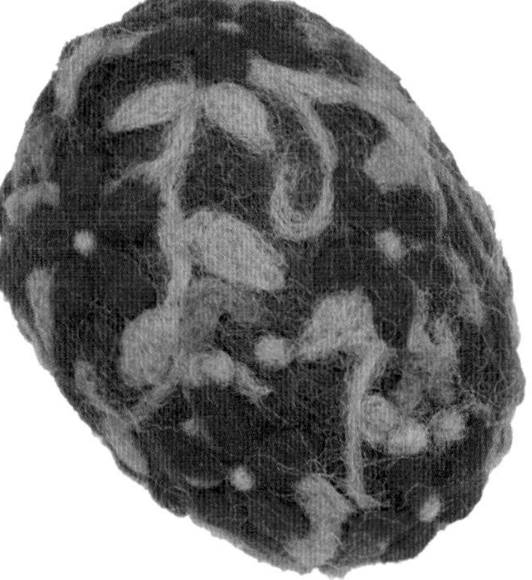

This project was completed with:

100% Corriedale wool in coordinating colors

Templates

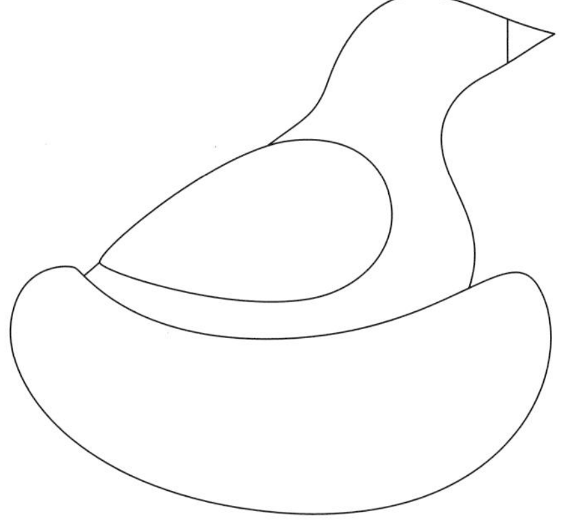

Nesting Photo Album
Enlarge as desired

Nesting Photo Album
Enlarge as desired

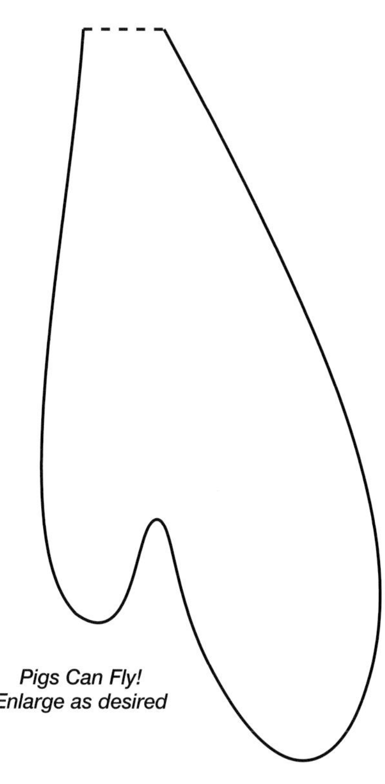

Pigs Can Fly!
Enlarge as desired

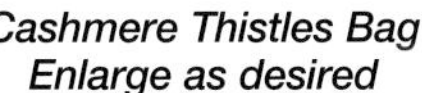

Cashmere Thistles Bag
Enlarge as desired

Passel of Puppies Pin
Enlarge as desired

Templates Continued

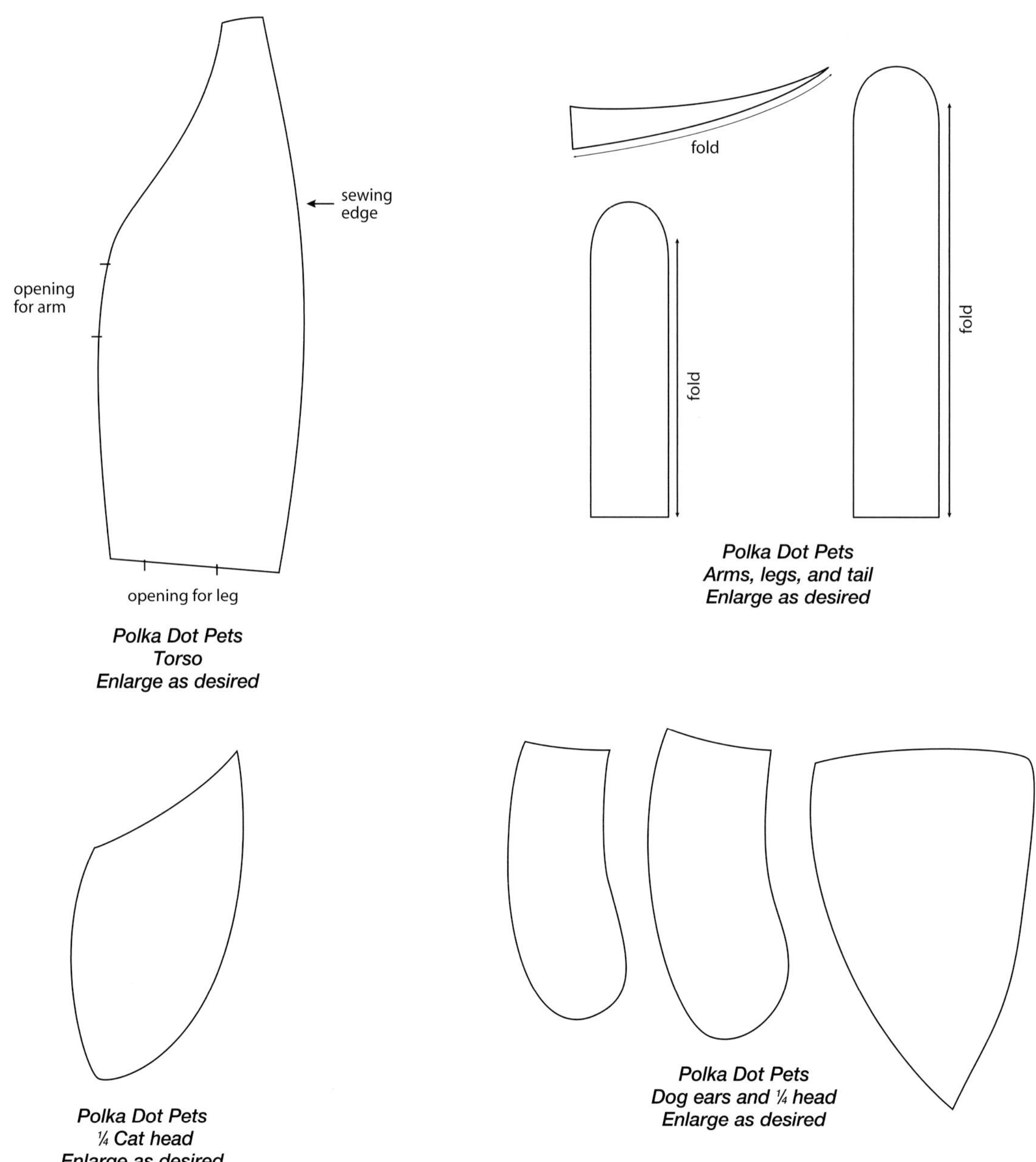

Polka Dot Pets
Torso
Enlarge as desired

Polka Dot Pets
Arms, legs, and tail
Enlarge as desired

Polka Dot Pets
¼ Cat head
Enlarge as desired

Polka Dot Pets
Dog ears and ¼ head
Enlarge as desired

Autumn Leaves Runner
Enlarge as desired

Oh la la Beret
Enlarge as desired

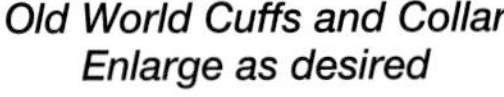

Old World Cuffs and Collar
Enlarge as desired

Marbles and Swirls Jewelry Pouch
Enlarge as desired

Designer Bios

Candie Cooper graduated from Purdue University, where she received degrees in Fine Arts and Art Education. Her passion lies in creating jewelry from unique materials and vibrant colors. She is the author of *Felted Jewelry: 20 Stylish Designs* (Lark Books, 2007). Candie's jewelry has been exhibited throughout the United States, England, and Europe. She lives and works in Shenzhen, China, with her husband Butch. Visit her website at www.candiecooper.com.

Barbara Crawford is the owner of Crawford Designs, an established pattern company that specializes in appliqué designs and country collectable dolls. She is also leading the way in the needle felting craze. Crawford Designs introduced the first two books in the U.S. on needle-felted wearables, fashion accessories, and dimensionals. Barbara travels the country as a teacher, speaker, and vendor. She has been designing since 1991, and in 1995 she established her pattern line for country collectable dolls. She was introduced to needle felting in 2005 and has been in love with it ever since. Visit her website at www.crawforddesigns.net.

Lisa Cruse has had an appreciation for the fiber arts since she created her first project at age 6. Her passion for color and design are now channeled into unique fiber arts projects. She has taught needlework, decorative painting, and traditional crafts to a varied audience over the years. She enjoys using fine art and faux effects in her work, to bring a unique style to her designs. Born in Michigan, Lisa now lives in the northwest corner of Connecticut with her daughter. You can view her work at www.lisacruse.com.

Longtime crafter **Nikola Davidson** discovered needle felting while visiting an alpaca farm in 2004 and was immediately obsessed. Inspired by the lack of needle felting kits on the market, she now creates her own through her business Sticky Wicket Crafts. Nikola has taught needle felting classes to introduce the craft to a wider audience. Part of the indie/DIY community in Seattle, she cofounded the Urban Craft Uprising in 2005 and helped to expand opportunities for urban crafters in the Northwest. She lives with her partner and two daughters. She is currently working on an Urban Craft Uprising book.

A weaver, spinner, dyer, and felter, **Linda Diak** has worked in fiber arts her entire life. She and her husband Tom live in Grafton, Vermont, with their three sons and a myriad of animals, including sheep, llamas, rabbits, chickens, and dogs. Linda and Tom own and operate Grafton Fibers, which supplies fiber enthusiasts with hand-dyed fibers and exquisite fiber tools. Look for them on the web at www.graftonfibers.com.

Marianne DuBois began wet felting in 1991 and was introduced to needle felting in 1995. She has been exploring it as a sculptural medium ever since. Her training as a geologist gave her an expert eye for creating three dimensional objects. Largely self-taught, Marianne has also taken classes with teachers like Sharon Costello, Ewa Kuniczak, and Brigitte Krag Hansen. She finds magic in using simple tools and wool to create sculptured forms. She runs Arcady Designs, her felting and teaching business, from a studio on the coast of Maine. Visit her website at www.hatmandu.com/arcadypage.htm.

L.K. Ludwig is a photographer and mixed-media artist living in western Pennsylvania. Her work has been shown in numerous galleries and magazines, including Somerset Studio, Belle Armoire, and Artitude. Her art has also been featured in *Making Journals by Hand* (Quarry, 2000), *The Altered Object* (Lark Books, 2006), and *Plush-o-Rama* (Lark Books, 2006).

Lindsay Obermeyer lives in Chicago, Illinois. Her grandmother taught her to knit and crochet. Lindsay teaches and has lectured extensively on fiber arts and needlecraft. She holds an M.F.A. from the University of Washington, an M.A.T. from National-Louis University, and a B.F.A. from the School of the Art Institute of Chicago. Her work has been shown in Boston's Museum of Fine Arts and the Milwaukee Art Museum, and can be viewed on her website at www.lbostudio.com.

Sandie O'Neill is an Australian textile artist who loves playing with natural fibers. Her interest in working with felt-making techniques developed out of a workshop she attended while managing a community college. She is passionate about teaching her skills to others and helping people get in touch with their artistic sides. Sandie lives with her husband and two daughters, and she considers herself a lifelong learner, as her family and students constantly teach her new things.

A pioneer in the field of machine needle felting, **Paula Scaffidi** is both an artist and a teacher. She is experienced in a wide range of media and draws inspiration from the natural world and the imagination. Exploring creative possibilities, Paula enjoys developing fresh textile techniques. With dual degrees in art and art education, she teaches nationally and offers creative textile retreats in North Carolina. She has also published articles in several countries. To learn more about Paula's art, go to www.fiberella.com.

Cooky Schock is the owner of The Shepherdess, a craft shop in San Diego that sells beads and crafting materials, as well as custom-made jewelry. Cooky teaches a variety of craft classes at the store. She enjoys felting and likes using the technique as a means of embellishment. To view her work and see a full listing of current classes, visit her website at www.shepherdessbeads.com.

Patricia Spark holds an M.F.A. from the University of Washington. She is a practicing artist in feltmaking, watercolor, monotypes and drawing. Her work has been shown nationally and internationally. She has written several books, including *The Watercolor Felt Workbook* and *Fundamentals of Feltmaking.* Patricia, a university art professor for 16 years, currently teaches workshops in felting and design. She taught for the Central Asian Craft Support Association (Bishkek, Kyrgyzstan 2006); at the World Symposium of Traditional and Contemporary Felt Art (Lakitelek, Hungary, 2004); the Georgian International Felting Conference (Tbilisi, Republic of Georgia, 1999), and the International Felting Festival (Korrö, Sweden, 1990). She is also the editor of the North American Felters' Network, a triannual publication for felt enthusiasts.

Marie Spaulding is a visual artist who enjoys working with wool and objects found in nature. She uses wet felting techniques and needle felting to create her handmade felt pieces, which include felted vessels, wall hangings and unusual wool sculptures. In 2004, Marie launched www.livingfelt.com, which features instructional kits and booklets on felting and needle felting. She has been featured on the DIY network, hosts an online felting community, and shows her work at art exhibits and galleries. You can view her work at www.mariespaulding.com.

Suzanne Urban graduated from a liberal arts college with a B.A. in studio art. She has been needle felting since 2001, and her sculpted wool figures have won honors at craft fairs around the country. Her goal is to see how far she can push the medium of needle felting by creating whimsical wool characters. Her work has been seen in Doll World, Contemporary Doll Collector, Doll Castle News, and other publications. Suzanne lives in Connecticut with her antiques dealer husband Mike. Her work can be viewed at www.smirkinggoddess.com.

Betz White is an artist with nearly two decades of design experience in the apparel industry. She applies the ancient art of felting to contemporary castoff sweaters to create projects that she describes as "felted wool, artfully stitched." With a flair for wit and whimsy, her designs reflect the everyday object in a fresh and humorous light. An avid knitter, sewer, and felter, Betz sells her one-of-a-kind recycled wool items internationally. She teaches workshops and maintains a popular blog (www.betzwhite.com).

Index